Inclusive Education and Disability in the Global South

Leda Kamenopoulou
Editor

Inclusive Education and Disability in the Global South

palgrave
macmillan

Editor
Leda Kamenopoulou
School of Education
University of Roehampton
London, UK

ISBN 978-3-319-72828-5   ISBN 978-3-319-72829-2   (eBook)
https://doi.org/10.1007/978-3-319-72829-2

Library of Congress Control Number: 2018933825

This Palgrave Macmillan imprint is published by Springer Nature
The registered company is Springer International Publishing AG
The registered company address is: Gewerbestrasse 11, 6330 Cham, Switzerland

This book is dedicated to my family,
especially:
yiayia Georgia,
Marina, Kostis,
Marcelo, Elektra,
and Leonardo!
Leda K.

PREFACE

I am honoured that I was given the opportunity to write this preface and to point out the importance of this book. This book makes a significant contribution to today's debates on inclusion in a school for all and in the development of global perspectives on inclusion, based on research-informed knowledge. Safeguarding all children's right to education and including them in the mainstream school is the key challenge faced by today's schools around the world. This book is timely because it reflects and highlights factors that facilitate or hinder education in a school for all within very different contexts.

According to UNESCOs' vision, access to education for all should be a human right and a goal in education policy for all countries. However, many contexts still have a long way to go in terms of reaching this goal, especially the global South countries covered in the four chapters (Chaps. 2–5) of this book that present research from Malaysia, Buthan, Philippines and Belize. Hence this book addresses current issues and themes related to the realisation of the vision of inclusive education as seen from a global South perspective, on which very little is known. The introductory chapter (Chap. 1) and the final chapter (Chap. 6) address generic and comprehensive issues that are relevant and important in all countries' efforts to develop inclusive education.

Chapter 1 is central to the inclusion debate, giving the overview of key terms like 'inclusion' and 'disability' and 'inclusive education' and 'special education'. Key perspectives related to disabilities and inclusion are highlighted to form the basis of the content of Chaps. 2 to 5 representing some experiences and practices of the global South. Chapter 2, which

focuses on the interaction of deafness and ethnicity in the process of identity development, addresses a very important topic in work involving
inclusion of students with special needs, which is how deaf people develop
their identity and what factors and experiences help shape their identity. In
line with previous research, the main findings of the chapter are that disability status means more than ethnicity in the development of identity
within the Malaysian context. Awareness of these findings can provide
deeper insight to different pupils' needs and a better understanding of
how to develop inclusive practices. Chapter 3 discusses the perceptions of
teachers about disabilities and inclusion in Bhutan and indicates how lack
of knowledge as well as inaccurate perceptions of disabilities, may shape
negative attitudes that do not promote inclusion. In the debate about
pathological perspectives within the special education field it is important
to reflect on how different understandings of disability influence attitudes
and behaviours towards inclusion. Therefore this chapter provides important information that will help professionals to reflect on how to meet
similar barriers. Chapter 4 regards the differentiated strategies that teachers use in the Philippines in order to assess pupils with disabilities as a basis
for adapting teaching to individual needs. The chapter offers insight to
different assessment strategies for all children and will help teachers to
improve their practice with respect to all pupils with and without disabilities. Chapter 5 presents the perspectives of teachers in Belize, who work
with visual impairment and blindness in mainstream schools, and offers
useful examples of different teaching strategies that allow teachers to
include visually impaired and blind pupils. Chapter 6 draws the thread and
connections between Chaps. 2–5. The strength of this chapter is the comprehensive framework developed by the author, in order to theorise inclusive education within global South contexts, and provides a helpful way of
systematising and understanding different aspects and topics within the
wider inclusion debate. Finally, it is relevant to note that although all
chapters are important to read in order to understand the book in its
wholeness, it is also possible nevertheless to read Chaps. 2–5 separately
since they are written independently and each focuses on a different
research project, undertaken within a particular global South context.

I highly recommend this book to practitioners, researchers and students in higher education in the field of inclusion.

Professor of Special Education and Inclusion   Jorun Buli-Holmberg
University of Oslo, Norway
September 2017

ACKNOWLEDGEMENTS

Exactly 5 years ago, I was embarking on an adventure that was destined to shape my research interests and work profoundly, by becoming the lead academic coordinator of the Erasmus Mundus Master's degree in Special and Inclusive Education (EMSIE). This postgraduate programme for teachers and other education professionals was unique in many ways, but mainly because it was the first of its kind (i.e. on the subject of inclusive and special education) to be offered jointly by three different European universities, i.e. the University of Roehampton, where I am based, and the Universities of Oslo in Norway and Charles in the Czech Republic. The project was funded by the European Union's Education, Audio-visual and Culture Executive Agency (EACEA) for five years and ran between 2011 and 2016, thus providing the opportunity to five selected cohorts of students from around the globe to deepen their knowledge on inclusive education and special educational needs whilst living and studying in three different European countries over the course of sixteen months.

The aim of EMSIE was to support professionals from anywhere in the world, especially those from countries of the global South, to further their knowledge and develop skills that would enable them to implement inclusive education in practice within their contexts in sustainable ways. The response we had from potential students took us aback: for every place available we received 20 times more applications. Whilst painstakingly reading every single one of the hundreds of applications we received over the course of the programme, each year it became clearer to me that there is great need for more programmes like EMSIE, because the sad reality is that teachers in many countries around the world still lack opportunities for any type of further professional development relevant to inclusive education.

During those five years, in my capacity as the academic coordinator of this multifaceted project, I enjoyed meeting and collaborating with excellent colleagues from other Universities, but what I mostly enjoyed was the untainted enthusiasm, genuine passion and desire to make a real change that I saw in my students, who are contributors to this book. *I would like to warmly thank all of them* not only for their excellent contributions, but also for being an endless source of positive energy and motivation during the writing and editing of this book. I decided to create this book in order to honour their enthusiasm by disseminating some of the best examples of research projects in which I have been involved as the academic coordinator of EMSIE. Each chapter of this book presents a research study that is both first class and ground breaking, and adds some important new knowledge on topics and contexts that have remained so far unexplored in the field of inclusive education and disability.

I am confident that readers will find this book timely, useful and enjoyable!

London   Leda Kamenopoulou
August 2017

Contents

List of Acronyms and Abbreviations

BCVI	Belize Council for the Visually Impaired
BIM	Bahasa Isyarat Malaysia (Malaysian Sign Language)
BSL	British Sign Language
CBR	Community Based Rehabilitation
CRC	Convention on the Rights of the Child
CRPD	Convention on the Rights of Persons with Disabilities
DepEd	Department of Education
EACEA	Education, Audiovisual and Culture Executive Agency
EFA	Education for All
EMSIE	Erasmus Mundus Master's in Special and Inclusive Education
FCM	Federal Constitution of Malaysia
FSD	Federation School for the Deaf
GEM	Global Education Monitoring Report
GNH	Gross National Happiness
ICIDH	International Classification of Impairments, Disabilities and Handicaps
IDRM	International Disability Rights Monitor
IEP	Individual Education Plan
IRO	Itinerant Resource Officer
IYDP	International Year of Disabled Persons
KTBM	Kod Tangan Bahasa Malaysia (Manually Coded Malay)
MFD	Malaysian Federation of the Deaf
MoE/MOE	Ministry of Education
NaRCIE	National Resource Centre for Inclusive Education
NZSL	New Zealand Sign Language

OMS	Orientation and Mobility Skills
PDA	Penang Deaf Association
ROP	Retinopathy of Prematurity
SDG	Sustainable Development Goals
SEN	Special Educational Need
SEU	Special Education Unit
UKM	Universiti Kebangsaan Malaysia
UN	United Nations
UNESCO	United Nations Educational, Scientific, and Cultural Organisation
US	United States
VI	Visual Impairment
WHO	World Health Organisation
ZPD	Zone of Proximal Development

NOTES ON CONTRIBUTORS

Joycelyn Nair Azueta worked as a secondary Science teacher for seven years in Belize. In 2015, she received an Erasmus Mundus Scholarship and undertook the MA/Mgr. in Special and Inclusive Education in London, Oslo, and Prague. The focus of her dissertation thesis was on Belize teachers' perspectives about teaching visually impaired students in mainstream schools. She is currently working on developing inclusive strategies that can be realistically implemented in her country and she intends to pursue a doctorate on inclusive education in the near future.

Dawa Dukpa is Associate Lecturer in Special and Inclusive Education and Educational Psychology at the Paro College of Education, Royal University of Bhutan. He joined Paro College in 2010 and currently he is serving as the Programme Leader for Inclusive Education at the College. He has published several articles on inclusion, disability and education in peer reviewed national journals. His current research interests are centered on inclusion, disability and teacher education.

Leda Kamenopoulou is Senior Lecturer in Special and Inclusive Education at the University of Roehampton, in London, UK. Over the past 20 years, she has worked as a teacher in schools and has held various research and teaching roles in UK and overseas Universities. She has published articles on Special Educational Needs and Inclusive Education in high quality national and international peer reviewed journals. Leda's current research is centred on the implementation of inclusive education within different contexts.

Andrea Pregel is Programme Advisor for Social Inclusion and Disability at Sightsavers, UK. He is an inclusion professional with experience in disability, development, education, gender and health across Europe, Asia and Africa, and is the co-founder of the Global Observatory for Inclusion (GLOBI). He holds a Bachelor's degree in Sociology and Social Research from the University of Turin (Italy), and an Erasmus Mundus MA/Mgr. in Special and Inclusive Education from the University of Roehampton, the University of Oslo and Charles University.

Rolando Jr. C. Villamero is an Expert on a Mission on Inclusive Education at UNICEF Kenya and an International Fellow of Joseph P Kennedy Jr Foundation. A teacher by profession, he has 10 years experience working on inclusive education for children with disabilities in developing countries, specifically on the aspects of teacher training, differentiated instruction, and community mobilisation. He spearheaded, for example, community-based initiatives in the Philippines such as the Inclusion Caravan, which trained almost 10,000 pre-service teachers on inclusive education strategies.

LIST OF FIGURES

LIST OF TABLES

CHAPTER 1

Introduction: Setting the Scene

Leda Kamenopoulou

Abstract In Chap. 1, which is the introduction, the author sets the context and outlines the book's focus and objectives. The chapter begins with a clarification of the concepts *Inclusive Education*, *Disability* and *global South*, followed by a description of the book's contribution to knowledge and how it expands our current understanding of these concepts. As the author explains, the qualitative research studies presented in this book focused on four countries of the global South, where research on inclusive education and disability is scarce, and as a consequence very little is known about the participation of some of the most vulnerable children in education within these contexts. The author argues for the need to allow thus far ignored and silenced voices and contexts to be heard.

Keywords Inclusive education/inclusion • Disability • Special educational needs • Global South • Qualitative research

L. Kamenopoulou (✉)
University of Roehampton, London, UK

© The Author(s) 2018
L. Kamenopoulou (ed.), *Inclusive Education and Disability in the
Global South*, https://doi.org/10.1007/978-3-319-72829-2_1

1

1.1   BOOK FOCUS AND OBJECTIVES

Inclusion in education or *inclusive education* concerns the participation in education of all children and especially of the most vulnerable ones, i.e. those who have traditionally been either excluded or at risk for exclusion from the education system. *Disability* in education has historically been the focus of special education, which is concerned with specialised strategies, approaches or even settings for the teaching of children with disabilities. However, since the Salamanca Statement and Framework for Action on Special Needs Education (UNESCO, 1994) set the groundwork for the inclusion of children with Special Educational Needs and/or Disabilities (SEN/D) in mainstream schools, a lot has changed in many countries around the world, and as a consequence, in the current context of increasing universal commitment to the full participation of all children in education, it is commonly accepted that those with disabilities also have the right of access to mainstream education. As a result, *inclusive education, special education* and *disability* have become intertwined and are often regarded as synonymous, but it is worthwhile to remember that the latter two are only one of the several foci of the former (for a more extensive discussion of the relationship between these concepts, see Kamenopoulou, Buli-Holmberg, & Siska, 2015; and for an excellent historical overview, see Kiuppis, 2014). This book focuses on *inclusive education* and *disability* in countries of the global South although it is acknowledged that children with disabilities are only one aspect of the wider and multifaceted inclusion project.

Global South is a term used nowadays to describe contexts that have a history of economic and political disadvantage and that used to be called *Third world* or *developing countries*. Usually this refers to countries in Africa, Asia, South America, Middle East and the Pacific that struggle with post-colonialist structures and oppression, extreme poverty and inequality, conflict, displacement and immigration, pandemics and the consequences of climate change, to name but a few. However, it is useful to stress that research has shown that some of the problems faced by societies in the south hemisphere, such as for example poverty, injustice and inequality are also faced by people living in parts of the north hemisphere. Hence the term *global South* does not necessarily describe geographical location and *'there are pockets of the global South in the global North'* (Stienstra, 2015: p. 632). Similarly, Australia and New Zealand for example are in the south hemisphere, but are not considered underdeveloped. Nonetheless, at the same time as being one of the richest countries, Australia has many indigenous people, who live marginalised and in absolute poverty (see Altman, 2007). Accordingly, the term *global South* in this book is used to describe economically disadvantaged and extremely inequal contexts or spaces, where the intersections between characteristics like gender, poverty, race and disability more often than not lead to *discrimination, marginalisation* and perpetuated educational and social *exclusion.*

The World Health Organisation estimates that 80% of the worldwide population of people with disabilities live in countries of the global South (WHO, 2011). Nevertheless, the voices and stories from these countries have been significantly under-represented in research literature about inclusive education and disability to date. Most published research on the subject has focused on global North countries, like the United Kingdom and the rest of Europe, the United States, and Australia (Grech, 2013). Moreover, as I explain in more detail in the next section, the majority of the limited research that has focused on the global South has been done by researchers based in the global North, who in this way continue to control knowledge and impose their own theoretical models and understandings on contexts of which at best they have a very superficial grasp (Damiani, Elder, & Okongo, 2016; Grech, 2013). This becomes particularly problematic when the foci of the research are inclusive education and disability, which are both vague concepts that can be constructed and interpreted from many different points of view. In relation to this, Farrell and Ainscow (2002) remind us that inclusive education remains a much-debated concept, with various different views as to what it means, what it entails and how it can be implemented in practice. Mitchell has moreover argued that inclusive education is a concept mediated by *'cultural values and beliefs, levels of economic wealth, and histories'* (2005: p. 15). The same applies to the conceptualisation of disability that has been found to vary depending on the context (Kamenopoulou & Dukpa, 2017; Radindran & Myers, 2012; Riany, Cuskelly, & Meredith, 2016) or the theoretical perspective adopted (Llewellyn & Hogan, 2000; Reindal, 2008).

It is specifically in the context of researching inclusive education and disability within the global South that the above points help refocus our thinking of inclusive education as a process mediated by a range of contextual factors and continuously influenced by particular local circumstances and characteristics. It thus becomes crucial to explore these particular local circumstances, and Len Barton (1997) advises that it is important to understand the specific contexts, in which inclusive education is expected to take place, emphasising the need to *listen to voices* from those contexts. Others have argued for the need to support the development of inclusive practices in culturally relevant ways, such as for example by enabling teachers to reflect on their own understandings of inclusion and its meaning within their specific cultural contexts (see Hansen, 2012).

This book presents four research studies on inclusion and disability carried out in four global South countries, where research on this subject has been limited and as a consequence, very little is known. These studies gathered some rare voices from *Malaysia, Bhutan, Philippines*, and *Belize*. All those countries share a commonality, which is that they are currently in the process of developing and approving their first policies for inclusive education and attempting to figure out how to implement them in practice. The authors ask questions that are timely and relevant and allow the voices and perspectives of the local people to be heard when addressing their research questions. I argue for the value of these particular voices in the wider debate about inclusive education and disability in the global South, because they help highlight the mediating role of cultural beliefs, personal histories, and other local realities in the conceptualisation and operationalisation of inclusive education (Mitchell, 2005). These mediating factors should not be ignored by researchers, but should be meticulously documented and explored in depth.

This book therefore aims to show that current debates about inclusion and disability can benefit from all voices, because what is relevant in one context may not necessarily be relevant in other contexts. This is the reason why researchers must aim for a plurality of perspectives when studying inclusion in education, provided of course, that the research has been conducted *'in a systematic and self-critical manner'* (Farrell & Aiscow, 2002: p. 9). Allowing different voices to be heard encourages a cross-cultural view of inclusive education, helps us focus on what it actually means for different people in different contexts and provides helpful insights into how inclusion can be implemented sustainably in these contexts. Similarly, capturing the stories and perspectives of global South contexts allows us to explore and illustrate unique experiences of disability, inclusion and exclusion lived within these contexts, and helps the development of inclusive education in ways that are meaningful, because they are responsive to the needs of these specific contexts.

In a nutshell, this book is here to argue that in discussions pertaining to disability and inclusive education all voices are valuable and have the right to be heard, and particularly those voices and contexts that have been thus far *silenced* or *ignored*. Accordingly, the specific objectives of this book are to:

1. Stress the role of local and cultural realities and contexts in the interpretation and operationalisation of inclusive education for children with disabilities.
2. Contribute to the decentralisation of global North ideas and research literature on inclusive education and disability.
3. Provide material that will further support teacher development on inclusive education and disability within a range of contexts.

1.2   CONTRIBUTION TO KNOWLEDGE OR WHY IS THIS BOOK NECESSARY?

The most ratified treaty in the world is the Convention on the Rights of the Child (CRC) that was signed in 1989 and protects the rights of all children, including those with disabilities. Articles 28 and 29 specifically stipulate children's right to education. Disabled children's right to inclusive education has moreover been legally established in many countries since the UN Convention on the Rights of Persons with Disabilities (CRPD) was adopted in 2006.

The concept of inclusive education, i.e. participation in education of all and especially of the most vulnerable groups was also reflected in the 'Education for All' (EFA) goals that the international community adopted in the World Education Forum in Dakar, which placed great emphasis on the participation in education of children who are disadvantaged, vulnerable, and those in difficult circumstances (UNESCO, 2000), but did not specifically mention those with disabilities. However, inclusive education can be seen as 'the same project' (Booth, 1999: p. 165) as EFA in that they are both concerned with removal of barriers to participation in education Consequently, the EFA framework led to the adoption of inclusive policies and their translation to practices in many countries. The concept of inclusive education was also included in the recent Sustainable Development Goals (SDG) adopted by countries in September 2015 (UN, 2015), and specifically in the fourth goal calling for inclusive and equitable quality education for all. More importantly, the fourth goal for the first time explicitly mentions disability, thus putting it firmly on the map and holding countries accountable for achieving this goal vis a vis disabled pupils (Kuper & Grech, 2017).

Sadly the UNESCO Global Education Monitoring Report (GEM) that assesses the extent to which countries are meeting the UN global education targets has repeatedly identified that significant work is still required at universal level towards the realisation of those targets. Notably, some of the issues that remain to be addressed are common in global North and South countries, such as for example the current big gaps in teacher preparation and training for inclusive education at universal level (UNICEF, 2012). Another common challenge is that despite agreed international goals for inclusive education, research shows that there are different operationalisations of those goals across countries (for an example comparison of policies across different European countries, see Smyth et al., 2014; for an example comparison of two South American countries, see Vásquez-Orjuela, 2015). Despite these common issues, overall great differences exist between rich and poor countries, in relation to the type of challenges they face in the realisation of inclusive education. For example, global North countries struggle with overloaded curricula, teacher burnout, and poor retention of teaching staff, whereas global South countries are challenged by poverty, social and economic inequality, conflict and displacement (Kamenopoulou et al., 2015; Stubbs, 2008).

Accordingly, it can be argued that inclusive education acquires a very different meaning and a much wider scope in the latter contexts, where the priority usually is to include all learners in basic education rather than focusing only on the inclusion of those groups of learners with disabilities. Support for this view is found in Booth (1999), who argues for the irrelevance of the special needs education model in the context of global South countries. Similarly, Tikly and Barrett (2011) propose that in the context of low-income countries a social justice framework would be more useful for perceiving education quality. Therefore one has to acknowledge that in global South countries, the struggle with social inequality and human rights is still real, hence there are several groups of children in need, who can be described as vulnerable or at risk for exclusion such as children soldiers, displaced children or children victims of armed conflicts. Moreover, when considering the needs of the disabled children growing up in these deprived contexts, one can imagine the many possible intersections between various disabling factors, because disability in these contexts is frequently associated with poverty, inequality or even directly caused by conflict and displacement.

Despite the very particular characteristics of global South contexts and their unique complexities, as mentioned earlier, research on disability in these contexts has been limited and for the most part conducted from a global North perspective (Grech, 2011, 2013, 2015a, 2015b). The field of disability studies has been dominated by UK and US urban and wealthy, middle class researchers whose approaches have produced questionable findings, thus *'making the Global South fit into their dominant perspectives as opposed to learning about this complex and hybrid space in its own right, including its emergent disability perspectives and theory'* (Grech, 2015a: p. 11). Similarly, in the field of inclusive education, historically there seems to have been a common assumption that predominant Western theories about inclusion can be readily applied to other geographical contexts, that is, without taking local realities into account (Grimes, 2013). It is therefore imperative to include more perspectives from the global South when exploring the global South, and this should apply to both theory generation and data collection for empirical research.

In relation to theory generation, some scholars have advocated for the need to explore and make more use of theorists from the global South. Miles (1995, 2000, 2011) makes a persuasive case for the value that Eastern cultures and religious or philosophical beliefs can bring to modern debates about disability. In a nutshell, his argument is that academics from the global North can no longer silence or ignore alternative interpretations and models originating from contexts of the global South, because the latter can refresh and significantly strengthen the field of disability studies. One example is the notion of karma, a Buddhist concept, which has been found to influence the way some Eastern cultures perceive disability and what they think about inclusion (for an extensive discussion of the karmic model of disability, see Kamenopoulou & Dukpa, 2017). In her truly fascinating book, 'Southern Theory', Raewyn Connell (2007) criticises the use of sociological theories constructed from global North points of view in order to explore global South countries, and argues for the need to use the work of Southern theorists when trying to understand Southern contexts. In specific relation to disability studies, Connell (2011) stresses that it *'currently has the same global North focus as other fields of the social sciences. It too is in need of renovation by moving both empirically and conceptually to a world scale.'* (p. 1372). Since the majority of disabled people live in the global periphery as opposed to the global metropole (i.e. Western Europe and North America), she maintains, a recognition of their experiences will change the current shape of disability studies by helping the field move beyond metropole-defined understandings of disability. An excellent example of how Southern theory can help refresh our understandings of inclusive education is provided by Mykherjee (2017), who in line with Connell, outlines a philosophy of inclusive education based on the theoretical ideas of Tangore, an Indian scholar of the nineteenth century, who established the *'socially inclusive school'* (p. 539), a child-centred and community oriented model, attentive to the child's needs, as an alternative to the colonial schooling system that was too competitive.

In relation to empirical research, some studies have looked directly at how children with disabilities are included in education in global South contexts. I refer the readers to the *Disability and the Global South* journal, which is a peer reviewed and open access publication dedicated to disseminating high quality research focused on the Global South. Moreover, the *International Journal of Inclusive Education*, a leading peer reviewed academic journal in the field with a global audience, occasionally publishes research studies focused on specific global South contexts. For example, Kalyanpur (2011) looked at the EFA and inclusive education frameworks in relation to Cambodia and concluded that international guidelines can be both helpful and harmful for developing countries. Franck and Joshi (2017) focused on EFA and the SDGs in the context of Ethiopia and found that despite favourable attitudes of school staff, their inclusive practices were restricted by lack of training and resources. Furthermore, readers may be interested in the *Asian Journal of Inclusive Education* that mainly disseminates research from Asian contexts. For example, Tasnuba and Tsokova (2015) investigated Bangladeshi primary teachers' attitudes and concerns regarding the inclusion of children with disabilities in mainstream classrooms and identified the need for training, support and resources for inclusive education. Singh (2016) explored the inclusion of children with disabilities in the early years in India and discovered some negative teacher attitudes. It is also worth mentioning here a few more journals that frequently disseminate Southern research, such as for example, *Disability and Society*—e.g. Chataika, Mckenzie, Swart, and Lyner-Cleophas (2012) discussed the CRPD in relation to Africa and stressed the need for the creation of a network to bridge the research and practice gap in the region; *International Journal of Disability, Development and Education*—e.g. Brydges and Mkandawire (2016) explored the experiences of students with Visual Impairment (VI) in Nigeria and found both lack of support and negative discrimination; and *Journal of Educational Development*—e.g. Lynch et al. (2011) highlighted barriers to the inclusion of children with a Visual Impairment (VI) in Kenya. To sum up, the limited research relating to inclusion and disability in the global South has so far illustrated many different challenges that these contexts face in implementing inclusive education for pupils with disabilities.

Despite this growing body of research and theoretical literature capturing global South voices, an increasing number of academic articles on disability and the global South, disability and poverty, and disability and the SDGs, make a strong case for a better understanding of the thus far marginalised global South perspectives and for more research that captures these perspectives. For example, Opini (2016) conducted a document analysis of the curriculum of selected disability studies programmes available in Canada, and found a remarkable absence of voices from the global South and a *'Eurocentric dominance'* (p. 80). The author raises two crucial questions: if such a curriculum is relevant to the lived experiences of students from global South contexts and at the same time, what students from the global North learn about disability in other contexts. She argues that marginalised groups, especially from the global South must be made visible in the field of disability studies. In an article examining the disability and poverty nexus, Groce, Kett, Lang, and Trani (2011) highlighted the lack of robust data on how exactly disability and poverty are correlated, but pointed to promising new research designs that have started to capture specific evidence, such as for example the fact that disabled people from low and middle income countries tend to have poorer access to education than their non-disabled peers. Moreover, the literature has thus far mainly looked at (a) disability as a factor accentuating poverty and (b) poverty as a factor increasing the likelihood of disability, but Groce et al. (2011) point out that disability and poverty are interconnected in multidimensional ways, and call for a deeper understanding of the experience of disability within a specific country. In a recent special issue of the Journal of *Disability and the Global South* focused entirely on disability and the SDGs, Kuper and Grech (2017) argued that despite the specific mention of disability in five of the SDGs, including the fourth one that concerns education, a lot more must be done to ensure that disabled people are included in reality and not only on paper. Specifically: *'we need genuine and ongoing spaces for critical thought, for research that provides evidence on the extent to which inclusion is happening on the ground'* (p. 1064).

Accordingly, this book sets out to fill some of the current gaps in our knowledge about inclusion and disability from a global South perspective, and in doing so, it will also complement the wider literature that has captured international voices in relation to inclusive education and disability. I will mention here some key books that the readers might find useful, but this is by no means an exhaustive list. In their book 'From them to Us', Booth and Ainscow (1998) presented a study on inclusion and exclusion in eight countries with the aim of enhancing interest in the role of *'national and local policies and cultural and linguistic histories on educational practice'* (p. 1). The countries covered were: US, Scotland, New Zealand, Norway, the Netherlands,

Ireland, Australia, and England. Focusing on the same countries, Ballard (1999) edited a book entitled 'Inclusive Education: International Voices on Disability and Justice', exploring inclusive education and related issues in an international context. Voices of disabled people, their parents/carers, and those of the researcher and the teachers were included in the book. Armstrong, Armstrong and Barton's book 'Inclusive Education: Policy, Contexts and Comparative Perspectives' (2000) provided comparative perspectives of inclusive education. They presented a series of case studies from Ireland, Greece, US, France, England, and Sweden, and their aim was to show how discourses, legislation, policy and resources shape inclusion in different societies. David Mitchell's edited book 'Contextualising Inclusive Education' (2005) offers a consideration of broader issues in relation to inclusive education in a wider range of contexts, i.e. specific countries (England, Canada, US, and Australia) and regions (Western Europe, Asia, Latin America, South Africa, and the Middle East). Gabel and Danforth compiled a selection of case studies from both developing and developed countries in their book 'Disability & the politics of education: an international reader' (2008), including South Africa, Zimbabwe, India, China and Colombia. In a theoretical book critically discussing international developments in inclusive education, researchers based in Australia, Armstrong, Armstrong, and Spandagou (2010) also cover some global South countries, e.g. India. More recently, Grech and Soldatic edited a volume entitled 'Disability in the Global South: The Critical Handbook' (2016). This very interesting book focuses solely on disability in the global South and includes research from different countries like Sri-Lanka, Ethiopia, South Africa, and Venezuela. It moreover provides a useful framework for conceptualising disability within these contexts in order to decentralise Western ideas and to decolonise the field of disability studies. This extensive volume explores issues that relate to disability, like poverty, health, colonialism, violence against women, and thus brings to the fore context-specific factors that influence the way disability is perceived and supported (or not) within these specific countries.

Lat but not least, it is noteworthy that two things set apart the present book from work previously published on inclusion and disability in countries of the global South. Firstly, it is a collection of voices from selected countries, i.e. Malaysia, Bhutan, Philippines, and Belize on which very little is known. This is because there is a dearth of published research on inclusion and disability in these countries, and accordingly, this book fills existing gaps and expands our current knowledge on this topic. Secondly, as I will explain in the following section, this book gives a voice to education professionals from very different backgrounds; who undertook postgraduate research on inclusive education and disability and in this book share what they learned in terms of possibilities and challenges for their specific contexts. These are professionals with considerable practical experience in disability and inclusive education in global South contexts, but who have also taken a step further and explored the theoretical basis and research evidence in relation to inclusive education. They have moreover conducted their own research focusing on their contexts and in doing so have given a voice to themselves and to those contexts. Consequently, their unique perspectives provide lessons that will be useful to academics, researchers, students, teachers and others interested in this topic. Opini (2016) argues that *disability studies will be strongest and most meaningful if it offers an inclusive space for students, faculty, researchers, community, to engage/participate in* (p. 80), and this is what this book hopes to achieve. As I stressed at the beginning of the introduction, the central argument of this book is that those *contexts* that remain *unexplored* and those *voices* that remain *silenced* have an important role to play in the advancement of thinking and practice in the field of inclusive education and disability in the global South, to which this book aims to contribute.

1.3   A Brief Background: An Innovative Postgraduate Programme for Teachers

The Erasmus Mundus Master's degree in Special and Inclusive Education (EMSIE) was an international collaboration between the Universities of Roehampton, Oslo and Charles that ran between 2011 and 2016. The programme was conceived as a much-needed response to the lack of programmes available for teachers, who wish to further their knowledge on special needs, disabilities and inclusion. This lack of training programmes for teachers on inclusive education has been well documented in the literature and is a common problem in many countries (see for example, Erten & Savage, 2012; Frood, 2011; Kamenopoulou et al., 2015; Kamenopoulou & Dukpa, 2017; Lawson, Norwich, & Nash, 2013).

EMSIE provided a unique opportunity to teaching professionals from around the globe to gain first-hand insights into inclusion and exclusion in different geographical, socio-economic and political contexts. The programme content and structure supported cutting-edge thinking and the development of reflexive research, which is about investigating, and reflecting on and across different contexts (see Booth, 1999). Accordingly, students critically engaged with key issues in the field especially during the period of their dissertation research, the outcomes of which were to inform more sustainable and culturally appropriate professional development and practice, by extending and building on the students' prior knowledge and experience in the field. During their final stage of conducting their dissertation research, the students also had the opportunity to opt for a 2–3 month placement in our associate partner University in Penang, Malaysia.

Elsewhere I have provided an account of the teaching and learning approach adopted for EMSIE and I have explained how the programme encouraged students to *'engage with and reflect on their own cultural contexts in multiple ways'*, thus helping them explore *'new theories and practices in direct relation to their contexts'* (see Kamenopoulou et al., 2015: p. 3). The programme was targeted at a wide range of practitioners from different countries including policy-makers, managers, teachers and those working in other agencies such as non-governmental organisations advocating for the rights of people with disabilities. As a result of the international focus of the programme, students came from a range of different countries and continents. The different nationality backgrounds of our students were a truly remarkable feature of the programme, and it is worth highlighting that very few students came from countries where inclusive education is well advanced. Most came from global South countries that are still in the process of developing their first policies and attempting to implement them in practice.

As part of their final module, i.e. the dissertation, students had to conduct their own original research project on inclusive education. The majority of students chose to focus on one of the European contexts where the programme allowed them to be based, i.e. England, Norway and Czech Republic. However, after two consecutive cohorts of students, because of my research interests, I was 'drawn' to those students who wanted to explore inclusion policies, ideas and practices within global South contexts. The originality of the research that resulted from our collaborations is without doubt, because of the simple fact that we ventured into exploring countries that were previously unexplored in relation to inclusion and disability, like most countries of the global South. This is why I decided to take this work one step further and to create this book. Every chapter is based on a dissertation project undertaken by the first author. In order to prepare this edited collection, we used some of the material from the students' dissertations as the starting point, but we have had to entirely re-write together many sections, expand some, and correct or perfect others as relevant. In some cases, such as for example for the study in Bhutan presented in Chap. 3, we conducted additional data collection in order to complement the original findings and to further triangulate them.

1.4   Overview of Chapters

Chapter 2 is an ethnographic study that gathered the voices of deaf people in Malaysia in relation to what factors shape their identity. The first author of this chapter, Andrea Pregel was the first ever EMSIE student to opt for a 3-month placement at our associate partner, University Sans Malaysia (USM) in Penang. This meant that he spent the months of August, September and October in Malaysia designing and conducting this research project for his dissertation module under my supervision. It is important to note that this is the first study of this kind ever conducted in Malaysia, and as a result, it provided some useful insights into context-related issues. Throughout the chapter, we focus on the particular complexity of the Malaysian society and when discussing the main findings we stress the need to listen to the voices of local Deaf people about how they themselves perceive their identity within such a complex context, and how they experience and understand the wider educational and societal opportunities and/or challenges presented to them.

Chapter 3 describes a research exploring the meaning of inclusion and disability from the perspective of Bhutanese people. The first author, Dawa Dukpa, who undertook his dissertation project under my supervision is a lecturer in the Paro College of Education in Bhutan, and has been interested in the preparation of Bhutanese teachers for inclusive education. He therefore conducted his dissertation research on the topic of teacher preparation for inclusion in Bhutan. After the dissertation was completed, we decided to expand it further, and conducted a series of additional interviews with both teachers and other locals, because we wanted to reach more diverse groups. In this chapter, we report findings from interviews with a range of local people about their perception of inclusion and disability. Again, this is one of the rare studies ever conducted on this subject in the context of Bhutan, and yields some interesting findings about the way in which people in Bhutan perceive inclusion and disability, as well as the survival of traditional cultural beliefs associating disability with past life karma. We discuss these findings and their implications in the context of Bhutan.

Chapter 4 presents a research that gave a voice to mainstream teachers from Negros Oriental in the Philippines asking them to share their experiences and the strategies they use when assessing pupils with disabilities. As we explain in the introduction, there is very limited systematic research on assessment strategies used for pupils with disabilities in the context of the Philippines. The first author of this chapter, Rolando Jr. C. Villamero, is a former teacher who was based for many years in the same region of the Philippines, where the research took place, and has been a youth advocate for the inclusion of disabled pupils in education and a leader of innovative projects focused on making the education system more accessible for pupils with disabilities in the Philippines. We worked closely together in order to produce this chapter based on his dissertation research, conducted under the supervision of Associate Professor Ivar Morken at the University of Oslo. In discussing the findings, we highlight the particular characteristics of the Philippines education system that may hinder the adoption of inclusive approaches to assessment. We moreover document how even in difficult circumstances, there are things that teachers can do as part of their every day practice in order to maximise the academic outcomes of pupils with disabilities.

Chapter 5 reports on a research that gathered the views of teachers in Belize about children with a Visual Impairment (VI) in mainstream schools. The first author, Joycelyn Nair Azueta, is from Belize and has worked for many years as a special needs lecturer and teacher in this country. Research on inclusive practices in Belize is extremely scarce and in her dissertation research, she explored the teachers' perspectives, the strategies they use in practice and the challenges they face when teaching children with VI in this context. In reporting some of the key findings in this chapter, we highlight a series of context-specific issues, such as the dearth of teacher training on Braille or the lack of early years support for orientation and mobility skills.

Finally, in Chap. 6 I bring together the most significant themes emerging from the four studies presented in the book, I highlight the key lessons learned and suggest ways forward in the field of inclusive education, disability, the global South and beyond. Based on my analysis of key themes emerging from the studies presented in the previous chapters, I put forward a simple theoretical framework for understanding inclusive education and the various concepts and issues that relate to it, and I argue that this framework can be particularly useful when thinking about possibilities and challenges for inclusion within global South contexts. This final chapter is underpinned by the central argument of the book, namely, that the field of inclusive education can benefit from research that explores and listens to the voices and perspectives of people and contexts that have thus far remained silenced and ignored.

When reading the chapters of this book, readers should look out for rare pieces of context specific knowledge that emerged from each of the studies. As a result they will have the unique opportunity to get a snapshot of each context and learn more about some of the realities and challenges as well as the opportunities for inclusive education in Malaysia, Bhutan, Philippines and Belize. Readers will be able to listen to the voices of local people, who took part in the studies presented, and to learn from their first hand experiences of disability, inclusion and exclusion in their contexts. At the same time, readers who are familiar with the broader field of inclusive education and disability will no doubt also begin to identify some more generic themes that are frequently found in the relevant literature regarding the barriers, challenges, opportunities, and hopes in relation to ensuring access to quality education for all. I will expand on these points in more detail in Chap. 6.

References

Altman, J. C. (2007). Alleviating poverty in remote Indigenous Australia: The role of the hybrid economy. *Development Bulletin, 72*, 1–9.

Armstrong, A. C., Armstrong, D., & Spandagou, I. (2010) *Inclusive education: International policy & practice*. London: SAGE Publishers.

Armstrong, F., Armstrong, D., & Barton, L. (Eds.). (2000). *Inclusive education: Policy, contexts and comparative perspectives*. London: David Fulton Publishers.

Ballard, K. (1999). *Inclusive education: International voices on disability and justice*. London: Falmer Press.

Barton, L. (1997). Inclusive education: Romantic, subversive or realistic? *International Journal of Inclusive Education, 1*(3), 231–242.

Booth, T. (1999). Viewing inclusion from a distance: Gaining perspective from comparative study. *Support for Learning, 14*(4), 164–168.

Booth, T., & Ainscow, M. (Eds.). (1998). *From them to us: An international study of inclusion in education*. London: Routledge.

Brydges, C., & Mkandawire, P. (2016). Perceptions and concerns about inclusive education among students with visual impairments in Lagos, Nigeria. *International Journal of Disability, Development and Education, 64*(2), 211–225.

Chataika, T., Mckenzie, J. A., Swart, E., & Lyner-Cleophas, M. (2012). Access to education in Africa: Responding to the United Nations convention on the rights of persons with disabilities. *Disability & Society, 27*(3), 385–398.

Connell, R. (2007). *Southern theory.* Cambridge: Polity Press.

Connell, R. (2011). Southern bodies and disability: Re-thinking concepts. *Third World Quarterly, 32*(8), 1369–1381.

Damiani, M. L., Elder, B. C., & Okongo, T. O. (2016). Tangible first steps: Inclusion committees as a strategy to create inclusive schools in Western Kenya. *Disability and the Global South, 3*(1), 865–888.

Erten, O., & Savage, R. S. (2012). Moving forward in inclusive education research. *International Journal of Inclusive Education, 162,* 221–233.

Farrell, P., & Ainscow, M. (2002). Making special education inclusive: Mapping the issues. In P. Farrell & M. Ainscow (Eds.), *Making special education inclusive* (pp. 1–12). London: David Fulton.

Franck, B., & Joshi, D. K. (2017). Including students with disabilities in education for all: Lessons from Ethiopia. *International Journal of Inclusive Education, 21*(4), 347–360.

Frood, K. (2011). The green paper—A view from mainstream. *Journal of Research in Special Educational Needs, 12*(2), 115–117.

Gabel, S. L., & Danforth, S. (2008). *Disability and the politics of education: An international reader.* New York: Peter Lang.

Grech, S. (2011). Comment from the field: Disability and the majority world: Challenging dominant epistemologies. *Journal of Literary and Cultural Disability Studies, 5*(2), 217–220.

Grech, S. (2013). Disability, childhood and poverty: Critical perspectives on Guatemala. In T. Curran & K. Runswick-Cole (Eds.), *Disabled children's childhood studies: Critical approaches in a global context* (pp. 89–104). Basingstoke: Palgrave Macmillan.

Grech, S. (2015a). *Disability and poverty in the global South: Renegotiating development in Guatemala.* London: Palgrave Macmillan.

Grech, S. (2015b). Decolonizing Eurocentric disability studies: Why colonialism matters in the disability and global South debate. *Social Identities: Journal for the Study of Race, Nation and Culture, 21*(1), 6–21.

Grech, S., & Soldatic, K. (Eds.). (2016). *Disability in the global South: The critical handbook.* Switzerland: Springer.

Grimes, P. (2013). Considering the continuing development of inclusive teachers: A case study from Bangkok, Thailand. *European Journal of Special Needs Education, 28*(2), 187–202.

Groce, N., Kett, M., Lang, R., & Trani, J.-F. (2011). Disability and poverty: The need for a more nuanced understanding of implications for development policy and practice. *Third World Quarterly, 33*(8), 1493–1513.

Hansen, J. H. (2012). Limits to inclusion. *International Journal of Inclusive Education, 16*(1), 89–98.

Kalyanpur, M. (2011). Paradigm and paradox: Education for all and the inclusion of children with disabilities in Cambodia. *International Journal of Inclusive Education, 15*(10), 1053–1071.

Kamenopoulou, L., Buli-Holmberg, J., & Siska, J. (2015). An exploration of student teachers' perspectives at the start of a post-graduate study programme on inclusion and special needs education. *International Journal of Inclusive Education, 20*(7), 743–755.

Kamenopoulou, L., & Dukpa, D. (2017). Karma and human rights: Bhutanese teachers' perspectives on inclusion and disability. *International Journal of Inclusive Education.* https://doi.org/10.1080/13603116.2017.1365274

Kiuppis, F. (2014). Why (not) associate the principle of inclusion with disability? Tracing connections from the start of the 'Salamanca Process'. *International Journal of Inclusive Education, 18*(7), 746–761.

Kuper, H., & Grech, S. (2017). Editorial: Disability and the SDGs: Is the battle over? *Disability and the Global South, 4*(1), 1061–1064.

Lawson, H., Norwich, B., & Nash, T. (2013). What trainees in England learn about teaching pupils with special educational needs/disabilities in their school-based work: The contribution of planned activities in one-year initial training courses. *European Journal of Special Needs Education, 28*(2), 136–155.

Llewellyn, A., & Hogan, K. (2000). The use and abuse of models of disability. *Disability and Society, 15*(1), 157–165.

Lynch, P., McCall, S., Douglas, G., McLinden, M., Mogesa, B., Mwaura, M., et al (2011). Inclusive educational practices in Kenya: Evidencing practice of itinerant teachers who work with children with visual impairment in local mainstream schools. *International Journal of Educational Development, 31*(5), 472–482.

Miles, M. (1995). Disability in an Eastern religious context: Historical perspectives. *Disability & Society, 10*(1), 49–70.

Miles, M. (2000). Disability on a different model: Glimpses of an Asian heritage. *Disability & Society, 15*(4), 603–618.

Miles, M. (2011). The 'Social model of disability' met a narrative of (in) credulity: A review. *Disability, CBR and Inclusive Development, 22*(1), 5–15.

Mitchell, D. (2005). Sixteen propositions on the contexts of inclusive education. In D. Mitchell (Ed.), *Contextualizing inclusive education: Evaluating old and new international perspectives* (pp. 1–21). London: Routledge.

Mukherjee, M. (2017). Educating the heart and the mind: Conceptualizing inclusive pedagogy for sustainable development. *Educational Philosophy and Theory, 49*(5), 531–549.

Opini, B. (2016). Walking the talk: Towards a more inclusive field of disability studies. *International Journal of Inclusive Education, 20*(1), 67–90.

Ravindran, N., & Myers, B. J. (2012). Cultural influences on perceptions of health, illness, and disability: A review and focus on Autism. *Journal of Child and Family Studies, 21*, 311–319.

Reindal, S. M. (2008). A social relational model of disability: A theoretical framework for special needs education? *European Journal of Special Needs Education, 23*(2), 35–146.

Riany, Y. E., Cuskelly, M., & Meredith, P. (2016). Cultural beliefs about Autism in Indonesia. *International Journal of Disability, Development & Education,* *63*(6), 623–640.

Singh, D. (2016). Dilemma and challenges of early education inclusion in schools of Lucknow, Uttar Pradesh, India. *Asian Journal of Inclusive Education,* *4*(1), 51–77.

Smyth, F., Shevlin, M., Buchner, T., Biewerb, G., Flynna, P., Latimierc, C., et al. (2014). Inclusive education in progress: Policy evolution in four European countries. *European Journal of Special Needs Education,* *29*(4), 433–445.

Stienstra, D. (2015). For Michael Charlie: Including girls and boys with disabilities in the global South/North. *Disability and the Global South,* *2*(2), 632–648.

Stubbs, S. (2008). *Inclusive education where there are few resources.* Oslo: Atlas Aliance.

Tasnuba, T., & Tsokova, D. (2015). BRAC primary school teachers' teaching-efficacy, attitude, sentiment and concern towards inclusion of children with disabilities in regular classrooms in Bangladesh. *Asian Journal of Inclusive Education,* *3*(1), 53–78.

Tikly, L., & Barrett, A. M. (2011). Social justice, capabilities and the quality of education in low income countries. *International Journal of Educational Development,* *31*(1), 3–14.

UN. (2015). *Transforming our world: The 2030 Agenda for sustainable development.* New York. Retrieved from https://sustainabledevelopment.un.org/content/documents/21252030%20Agenda%20for%20Sustainable%20Development%20web.pdf

UNESCO. (1994). *The Salamanca statement and framework for action on special needs education.* Paris, France. Retrieved from http://www.unesco.org/education/pdf/SALAMA_E.PDF

UNESCO. (2000). *The Dakar framework for action. Education for all: Meeting our collective commitments.* Dakar, Senegal. Retrieved from http://unesdoc.unesco.org/images/0012/001211/121147e.pdf

UNICEF. (2012). *The right of children with disabilities to education: A rights based approach to inclusive education.* Geneva: UNICEF CEECIS Regional Office.

Vásquez-Orjuela, D. (2015). Políticas de inclusión educativa: una comparación entre Colombia y Chile. *Educations and Educators,* *18*(1), 45–61.

World Health Organisation and World Bank. (2011). *World report on disability.* Geneva: WHO.

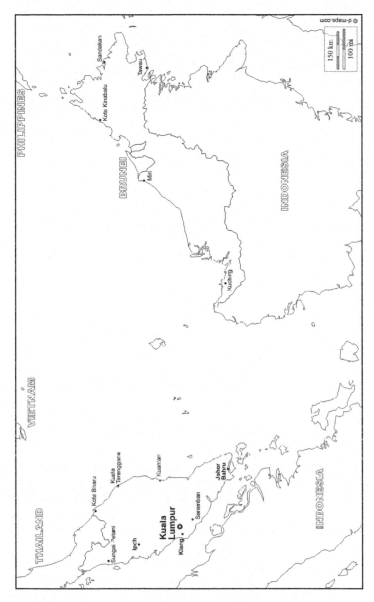

Fig. 2.1 Map of Malaysia (Source: http://www.d-maps.com/m/asia/malaisie/malaisie22.gif)

CHAPTER 2

The Interplay of Deafness and Ethnicity in Processes of Identity Development: An Ethnographic Study Within the Penang Deaf Community in Malaysia

Andrea Pregel and Leda Kamenopoulou

Abstract Chapter 2 presents the first research ever conducted on the interplay of deafness and ethnicity in the process of identity development in Penang, Malaysia. The authors used an ethnographic methodology to capture the voices of 4 deaf adults belonging to different ethnicities. Findings suggest that disability was more relevant than ethnicity in shaping individual and social identities within this particular context. Experiences of discrimination or belonging played a fundamental role in identity development, and these were primarily shaped by disability rather than ethnicity. For example, factors such as the lack of a common language between deaf children and hearing parents influenced children's sense of identity. However, the authors also stress that participants mainly saw their identities as fluid and context-dependent rather than static and non-changing.

A. Pregel (✉)
GLOBI: Global Observatory for Inclusion, Brighton, UK

L. Kamenopoulou
University of Roehampton, London, UK

© The Author(s) 2018   21
L. Kamenopoulou (ed.), *Inclusive Education and Disability in the Global South*, https://doi.org/10.1007/978-3-319-72829-2_2

Keywords Deafness • Ethnicity • Identity development • Sign language • Malaysia

> *"I am Indian. And I'm Hindu. And I'm deaf also.*
> *And I'm not only Deaf, I'm also hearing... half hearing."*
> (Amita)

2.1   INTRODUCTION

Research conducted in different countries shows that experiences within family, school, cultural and social environments have a significant impact on processes of identity development in deaf individuals belonging to minority ethnic groups, and in their inclusion within local Deaf and ethnic communities (Ahmad, Atkin, & Farhades, 2002; Ahmad, Darr, Farhades, & Nisar, 1998; Anderson & Grace, 1991; Anderson & Miller, 2004; Aramburo, 1989; Atkin, Ahmad, & Farhades, 2002; Foster & Kinuthia, 2003; James & Woll, 2004; Smiler & McKee, 2007; Davis & McKay-Cody, 2010; Woll & Ladd, 2010).

The research that we report here is the first study ever conducted on the interplay of ethnicity and deafness in Malaysia. As we discuss in the next section, the Malaysian society is multicultural in a unique way. We were therefore interested to explore the interplay of deafness and ethnicity in the process of identity development in such a multicultural context. We adopted an ethnographic approach with in-depth semi-structured interviews and participant observations to investigate the experiences and identity narratives of deaf people living in Penang and belonging to different ethnic groups. The research explored their processes of identity development in relation to their participation within family, school, social and cultural environments, and their inclusion within the Deaf and ethnic communities.

Deafness clearly emerged from our research as more relevant than ethnicity in shaping participants' individual and social identities in the specific context of Penang. Findings also indicated that both experiences of discrimination and belonging within family and other social environments play a fundamental role in processes of identity development. The lack of a common language among deaf children and hearing parents in ethnic minority households, for example, has a profound impact on children, their self-confidence and sense of identity. Overall, participants saw their identities as fluid, multicultural and contextual.

Data were collected in Malaysia over the course of three months by the first author. As the research focused on identity, the first author reflected on his own multiple identities and took into consideration issues of *reflexivity* and *positionality* (Edwards & Ribbens, 1998; Sultana, 2007), and we discuss these in detail later on. We would like to stress from the outset that we do not claim that results and interpretations contained in this chapter represent the absolute true version of social reality. In fact, we are strongly convinced that such true version does not exist. Admittedly, to some degree findings and conclusions presented here are products of the interactions between the researcher and the local informants, mediated through their personal perspectives. However, our aim is to allow the voices of the local informants to emerge from their narratives and to highlight their experiences and perspectives.

In the first section of this chapter we introduce the Malaysian context. The relevant literature, methodology and findings of our study are the focus of the second section. The third and final section provides some conclusions and recommendations.

2.2   Inclusion and Deafness in Malaysia

Malaysia is a country in Southeast Asia with an extremely multicultural society. Bumiputras (Bumiputra literally means *son of the land*, and includes ethnic Malays and aboriginal people of Sabah and Sarawak) constitute 68.6% of the population, followed by Chinese, 23.4%, Indians, 7.0%, and other ethnicities, 1.0% (Malaysian Department of Statistics, 2016). Bahasa Malaysia (Malaysian) is the official language spoken by the whole population; nonetheless, English, Chinese, Tamil, and several indigenous idioms are widely used across the country. Islam is the official and most popular religion (60.4%), followed by Buddhism (19.2%), Christianity (9.1%), Hinduism (6.3%), traditional Chinese cults (2.6%), other religions or nonreligious people (2.4%) (Central Intelligence Agency, 2009).

Due to a long history of colonialism and to the economic policies of the past four decades, the Malaysian society is highly stratified. Despite being a minority group, the Chinese community is extremely prosperous, controlling approximately 70% of the Malaysian economy (Chua, 2004); Malays represent the political majority, but still lack financial power

(Nakamura, 2002); Indians are at the bottom of the economic pyramid, often employed in rural areas or relegated to the manual labour market (Airriess, 2000).

In 1994 Malaysia signed the Salamanca Statement (UNESCO, 1994), and inclusive education for students with disabilities and/or special educational needs was introduced with the Education Act 1996 (Government of Malaysia, 1996), enabling their temporary or full integration into mainstream classrooms in primary and secondary schools (Ali, Mustapha, & Jelas, 2006). Malaysia signed the Convention on the Rights of Persons with Disabilities (CRPD) (United Nations, 2006) in 2008, and ratified it in 2010. Additionally, the Persons with Disabilities Act 2008 was approved (Government of Malaysia, 2008) to address issues of segregation and discrimination experienced by people with disabilities (Goodley & Lawthom, 2011). It is argued however that legislation has had limited impact on the daily life of people with disabilities (see for example Clark, Brown, & Karrapaya, 2012). Crowded classes, ambiguous policies, paucity of resources, and lack of collaboration with specialised services continue to be crucial barriers, and full inclusion is extremely limited (Wah, 2010).

There is no official census of deaf people in Malaysia. Estimates vary from 55,000 (Murad, 2013) to 66,000 deaf individuals (Hurlbut, 2000). Malaysian Sign Language (Bahasa Isyarat Malaysia—BIM) is the main language used by deaf people, although regional variations and dialects exist (Ethnologue, 2013). The Persons with Disabilities Act 2008 (Government of Malaysia, 2008) recognises BIM as the official sign language in Malaysia. It is relevant to note, however, that Deaf schools employ Manually Coded Malay (*Kod Tangan Bahasa Malaysia*—KTBM) as medium for instruction. This may have implications on students' learning and highlights how the process of full recognition of BIM as the language for deaf people in Malaysia is still far from being implemented (Abdullah, 2013).

The Malaysian Federation of the Deaf (MFD) is the leading Deaf organisation in the country, and has ten affiliated associations distributed in different states, while the Penang Deaf Association (PDA) is the chief organisation in Penang. There are 23 Deaf schools in Malaysia, but students with hearing impairments are also integrated in mainstream settings (Ghadim, Alias, Rashid, & Yusoff, 2013). The Federation School for the Deaf (FSD) (the original name is *Sekolah Menengah Pendidikan Khas Persekutuan*, meaning *Secondary School for Special Education*) was founded in Penang in 1954 with eight students, and was the first Deaf school in Malaysia (Lim, Woo, & Chong, 2006). Most deaf students choose vocational training after the completion of secondary school, and only a very small number of deaf people attend courses at university level, due to lack of academic qualifications and paucity of adequate support and resources (Jaafar & Mee, 2010).

2.3   THE INTERPLAY OF DEAFNESS AND ETHNICITY IN PROCESSES OF IDENTITY DEVELOPMENT

In this section we provide an overview of relevant literature on ethnic and deaf identities, and discuss empirical studies on the interplay of deafness and ethnicity. Subsequently, the methodology that we adopted for our study is presented, followed by a review of the main results and the discussion and interpretation of findings.

2.3.1   Review of the Literature

Identity
In the social sciences, different terms such as *identity*, *self-concept*, and *self-image* are frequently used interchangeably to define individuals' understanding and knowledge of themselves.

In Mead's (1934) perspective, identity is the result of the meanings that individuals associate to their multiple roles within differentiated societies, and language is a tool to convey shared symbolic meanings. Within symbolic interactionist perspectives, *meaning* is regarded as an individual product mediated through human interaction and a process of interpretation (Blumer, 1969), and identity 'stands in a dialectical relationship with society' (Berger & Luckman, 1971: p. 194).

Recently, Jenkins (2014) proposed the abandonment of static conceptions of self, and the acknowledgment of its processual nature. This view is consistent with postmodern approaches to social reality, which is seen as a complex structure where multiple meanings and competing discourses interlace and coexist (Lyotard, 1984). Accordingly, the self is conceived as a fluid dimension, and plural identities are constantly constructed, destroyed and rebuilt in a rich multicultural social landscape (Leigh, 2009).

Ethnic Identities
Ethnicity, is commonly used as an umbrella classification that 'embraces groups differentiated by colour, language, and religion; it covers "tribes,"

"races," "nationalities," and castes' (Horowitz, 1985: p. 53). Ethnic boundaries have a fluid nature and change across generations: in order for them to persist, social arrangements and cultural practices (e.g. languages, religions, food, traditional clothes, etc.) must be consolidated (Hirschman, 1987). Chandra further describes ethnicity as 'a subset of identity categories in which eligibility for membership is determined by descent-based attributes' (2006: p. 400). Within this framework, therefore, the notion of ethnicity applies to groups, which are larger than families, have recognised common ancestry, are conceptually autonomous, and for which belonging is determined by descent.

It is relevant to note here that within the Malaysian context there is a strict link between ethnicity, language, and religion, and there is vast heterogeneity within ethnic groups. However, article 160 of the Federal Constitution of Malaysia (FCM) (2010) clearly states that 'Malay means a person who professes the religion of Islam, habitually speaks the Malay language, conforms to Malay custom' (p. 153). Airriess (2000) underlines that Malaysia made considerable efforts to create a harmonious multicultural society, however, 'to claim that ethnic animosity has been eliminated is short-sighted' (p. 345).

Deaf Identities

Deaf people use different expressions to define themselves: *Deaf, hearing impaired, hard of hearing,* and *deafened* represent the most commonly used terms (Ahmad et al., 1998; Byrne, 1998; Kirk, Gallagher, Coleman, & Anastasiow, 2011). In the context of Deaf Studies, a dichotomy between *deaf* and *Deaf* is traditionally adopted to discuss issues of identity, membership, and belonging (Woodward, 1972). Within this framework, 'to be deaf is to have a hearing loss; to be Deaf is to belong to a community with its own language and culture' (James & Woll, 2004: p. 125). On the one hand, *deafness* is regarded as an impairment or a pathology, and is framed in the context of *oralism* (e.g. use of hearing aids, cochlear implants, lip-reading, etc.) (Napier, 2002); on the other hand, *Deafness* is conceived as a cultural trait, and refers to individuals belonging to the Deaf community and using sign language (Mascia & Mascia, 2012). In this chapter *Deaf* is used to refer to Deaf communities, Deaf culture, Deaf Studies, and Deaf Education, and *deaf* to refer to deafness in general terms. When discussing research of other authors, their terminology is adopted.

Decades of struggles, oppression, isolation, and fights favoured the development of Deaf communities around the world, built upon shared

Deaf cultures, collective Deaf identities, a sense of Deaf pride, and the use of sign languages (Atkin et al., 2002; Erting & Woodward, 1979; Ladd, 2003; Lane, Hoffmeister, & Bahan, 1996; Scott-Hill, 2003; Stebnicki & Coeling, 1999; Woll & Ladd, 2010; Wrigley, 1996). Ladd (2003) further proposes the concept of *Deafhood* to describe the sum of all the objective meanings and values of a collective concept of Deaf culture, as well as the personal pursuit of identity of each Deaf individual. Within this framework, the notion of Deafhood describes the potential existence of a global Deaf identity, capable of reaching beyond national boundaries (Ladd & Lane, 2013).

In relation to this, the double d/Deaf definition is generally adopted in Malaysia (Jaafar & Mee, 2010); however, Ladd and Lane (2013) argue that 'what we in the West understand as capital-D Deaf characteristics do not necessarily apply to non-Western Deaf communities and cultures' (p. 574). The use of hearing technologies such as cochlear implants is extremely spread in Western countries, where approximately 80% of deaf children get implanted (Humphries et al., 2012). However, cochlear implants are quite rare in Malaysia: the first Cochlear Implant Programme started in 1995 at Universiti Kebangsaan Malaysia (UKM) (Umat, Siti, & Azlizawati, 2010), and only 295 individuals successfully received the implant during the following 15 years (Lim, 2011). As previously discussed, the majority of deaf children in Malaysia go to Deaf schools, learn sign language and become part of the Deaf community.

The Interplay of Deafness and Ethnicity
An increasing number of studies have been conducted in recent years in relation to what could be described as *sub-communities* of the wider national Deaf communities (Woll & Ladd, 2010). Sometimes these sub-communities operate harmoniously within the main Deaf community; on other occasions, however, they become an oppositional minority within the major Deaf community, as is the case of the Black Deaf community in South Africa and United States during the era of racial segregation (Woll & Ladd, 2010).

One of the first seminal studies on the interplay of ethnicity and deafness was conducted by Aramburo (1989), who surveyed sixty members of the black deaf community in Washington D.C. The study collected enough evidence of the actual existence of a deaf black community, separated both from the deaf community and the black community, and 87% of the respondents identified themselves as black first and were more competent in relation to aspects of the black culture, rather than the deaf culture. On the other hand, 13% of the participants identified themselves as deaf first: most of the respondents within this group had deaf parents and attended a residential school for the deaf. Furthermore, all respondents declared that they felt discriminated because of their colour, their deafness, or both. Several individuals stated that they felt discriminated also by members of the deaf community, due to their black skin, and by hearing members of the black community. Members of the black hearing community and the (white) deaf community, therefore, appeared to be at the same time *discriminated* by the wider community, and *discriminating* members of a smaller sub-culture.

Reviewing relevant research and professional literature on Black deaf adolescents, Anderson and Grace (1991) argue that they could be described as a *minority within a minority*. Among various obstacles, the authors particularly underline the repercussion of stereotypes, discrimination and prejudice, and the absence of Black deaf role models. Furthermore, they highlight individuals' need to deal with a variety of values and norms: those of their cultures, and those of the larger and dominant culture.

Results of a study conducted with 70 South Asian deaf youngsters and 15 hearing family members living in the UK are reported in Ahmad et al. (2002) and Atkin et al. (2002). The lack of a common language within the family environment often had two relevant consequences: the inability of parents to communicate their religious and cultural values and their children approaching the wider white Deaf community. This practice was not highly regarded: parents often saw Deaf culture in contrast to their own religious and cultural values, and in some cases attempted *normalisation strategies*, forbidding their children from using the British Sign Language (BSL). These parents struggled in accepting their children's diversity, and saw Deaf identity as an extension of the dominant white Christian identity. As a consequence, several youngsters had difficulties in sustaining self-confidence and a positive self-image. They demonstrated only partial understanding of their religions, and their 'reluctance to attend mosques or temples was resented by parents' (Atkin et al., 2002: p. 33). Interestingly, youngsters held plural identifications, such as Asian, Deaf, and Muslim, and used them flexibly in different contexts (Ahmad et al., 2002).

Research has also explored the identities and cultural affiliations of Deaf Native Americans. Woll & Ladd (2010) cite research noting that Deaf Native Americans often feel isolated and alienated in their interactions with hearing Native individuals, and they experience 'limited participation within Native American culture, and difficulty in maintaining their Native American identity in the wider Deaf community' (p. 161). Furthermore, Davis and McKay-Cody (2010) point out that many Deaf Natives encounter cultural barriers within residential schools for the deaf, where the observance of cultural habits and traditions of Native American tribes are often discouraged or prohibited.

Foster and Kinuthia (2003) investigated processes of identity development of deaf college students belonging to minority ethnic groups in the US. The theme of difference recurred in many interviews: as the authors note, realising to be similar and connected to others can be powerful in shaping identity, but 'difference in the form of social alienation can lead to deep isolation and the inability to find or establish a sense of identity' (p. 280). The authors drew on Stryker's (1968) notion of *identity salience*, defined as the likelihood that a certain identity will be invoked by a person in different contexts, and results of the study indicate that the participants did not conceive identity as a static attribute: rather, identity appeared as fluid, dynamic, responsive and contextual.

Anderson and Miller (2004) collected biographies of multicultural Deaf persons in the US. Analysing those stories, they observe that those individuals shared common experiences of interaction in multiple cultures: all the participants, in fact, faced similar challenges within families, schools, peer groups, and had to overcome multiple forms of stereotypes and discrimination. Furthermore, a key element emerging from the biographies was the importance of multicultural Deaf mentors and adult role models. The authors note that 'the contributions of childhood and family life experiences are essential in the development of a positive self-identity and self-esteem' (p. 33).

James and Woll (2004) discuss the results of a study conducted in London with British Black Deaf individuals of African or Afro-Caribbean origin. Lack of communication within the family emerged as the major cause of some participants' feeling of isolation, and lack of awareness of their cultural and racial heritage. Many informants also described episodes of racism at school (both mainstream and Deaf schools), and complicated relationships with teachers, which were often white and hearing. All participants faced challenges in relation to employment; most of them felt discriminated because they were deaf, but some believed that racism was a further obstacle. Participants had mixed opinions about the existence of an actual Black Deaf community, also due to the absence of Black Deaf role models, which 'made some informants feel that a 'Deaf Apartheid' existed, fuelled by inter-ethnic antagonism between different Deaf minority groups' (p. 147). In terms of individual identities, some informants defined themselves as Black Deaf, mainly communicated in spoken English and had closer connections with the Black hearing community. Others described themselves as Deaf Black, and strongly belonged to the Deaf community. Some others felt that Deafness and Blackness were equally important attributes, and negotiated their multiculturalism according to the context.

Finally, Smiler and McKee (2007) explored *Māori* Deaf people's perceptions of identity in New Zealand. All participants described socialisation with Deaf peers at school, the use of New Zealand Sign Language (NZSL), as well as instances of exclusion in hearing schools and within home environments as fundamental steps in the development of Deaf identity. Nonetheless, being educated in a predominantly mono-cultural (hearing and non-*Māori*) education system, all participants reported a common sense of alienation. Interactions with hearing family members were also complicated, and resulted for most participants in a weak sense of *Māori* identity. Results of the study suggest that experiences of alienation and exclusion, on the one hand, and inclusion and affinity, on the other hand, exercise a robust influence on the processes of identity development. Access to 'meaningful social and linguistic interaction with peers and role models' (Smiler & McKee, 2007: p. 101), both in the Deaf and the *Māori* world, was highlighted as a key factor for the development of plural identities. An extremely relevant finding of the study is that participants did not identify with one unique primary element of identity: on the contrary, some of them explicitly rejected 'the notion of primacy between facets of identity that are non-negotiable and equally important for social survival in various contexts' (p. 102). Within this perspective, identity can be described as a constellation of different elements that are more or less relevant, depending on the context.

2.3.2   Methodology

Research Approach and Theoretical Framework
The aim of our research was to collect narratives of deaf individuals belonging to different ethnic groups and to explore their processes of identity development. The research was initially framed within a constructivist ontological approach, and interpretivism was the natural epistemological choice. From a constructivist viewpoint, reality is socially constructed (Berger &

Luckmann, 1971): it cannot be *discovered*, but only *understood*, as it does not exist before its construction (Hartas, 2010). Additionally, interpretivism maintains that individuals experience reality in distinctive ways and attribute different meanings to social phenomena (Bryman, 2012).

Symbolic interactionism is one of the major theories emerged from interpretivist epistemologies and represented a relevant theoretical framework for this research. According to Blumer (1969), symbolic interactionism is shaped by three fundamental ideas: first, individuals interact with the external world according to the meanings that the external world has for them; second, these meanings originate from the interactions among individuals; and third, these meanings are negotiated and modified by each human being during the process of interaction with the external word. Postmodernism represented another important point of reference in our investigation: according to postmodernist approaches to identity development, the self is constructed as a fluid dimension and individuals elaborate coexisting plural identities to deal with a multi-layered social reality (Lyotard, 1984).

Drawing upon a constructivist ontology and being interested in individual interpretations of reality, we adopted a *qualitative approach* in this study. Qualitative research employs an *emerging design* and is based on an *inductive process* (Bryman, 2012), as conceptual categories are elaborated during the analytical process (Cohen, Manion, & Morrison, 2007). Our research, therefore, could be described as an *interpretive study* (Maxwell, 1996) that seeks to 'explore peoples' experiences and their views or perspectives of these experiences' (Gray, 2014: p. 37).

Research Methods, Participants and Procedures
In-depth semi-structured interviews framed within a narrative approach constituted the main research method in this study. Participant observations conducted in schools and within the Deaf community were a secondary source of data.

Semi structured interviews are characterised by flexible open-ended questions: these are particularly appropriate to investigate individuals' interpretations of social reality as expressed in their own languages, words, and voices (Byrne, 2012). Additionally, the narrative approach enables informants to organise personal experiences 'with continuity through time' (Elliott, 2005: p. 126), and is valuable to collect narratives, which could be described as 'ways in which we make sense of our lives' (Lodico, Spaulding, & Voegtle, 2010: p. 147).

Four participants were selected for the interviews through purposive sampling. *Deafness* was a fixed parameter for the sample construction: all participants had to be deaf. The second parameter, however, was *ethnicity*: in relation to this element, maximum variation sampling was employed, in the attempt to include the highest possible degree of diversity among participants (Lodico et al., 2010). Other parameters included *religion, age, gender, education,* and *employment.*

As discussed in the literature review, previous studies on deafness and ethnicity have mainly focused on minorities. In the state of Penang, however, the majority of the population is ethnic Chinese, and ethnic Malays are a minority in their own country. For this reason, one ethnic Malay was included in the sample. The final sample included one Malay, one Chinese, one Indian, and one Eurasian native of Sabah. Participants' profiles are reported in Table 2.1. For descriptive purposes, the following two operational definitions are adopted when referring to ethnicity in some parts of this study: *large minorities,* comprising Malays, Chinese, and Indians; and *small minorities,* referring to Eurasians and other aboriginal people.

All interviews were conducted by the first author in environments selected by the participants, using BIM with the help of a certified interpreter, and were video-recorded. The first author had previous knowledge of two sign languages and took BIM classes in Penang. Learning BIM proved to be an invaluable way of interacting with Deaf people. This familiarity with the Deaf community was crucial in order to identify informants (Lodico et al., 2010) and gatekeepers (Cohen et al., 2007), such as members of the main Deaf organisations, interpreters, teachers, and Deaf advocates, and ultimately, participants for the interviews.

Participant observations were conducted in the Penang Deaf community in support of the interviews by the first author. The role of the researcher

Table 2.1 Participants' profiles

	Zara	Ana	Amita	Farhad
Hearing status	Deaf	Deaf	Deaf	Deaf
Ethnicity	Eurasian	Chinese	Indian	Malay
Age group	25–31	25–31	25–31	25–31
Gender	Female	Female	Female	Male
Religion	Christian	Christian	Hindu	Muslim
Education	College	College	College	University
Employment	Teacher	Self-employed	Teacher/coordinator	–

was known and clear, and during the observations he took actively part in some activities. Therefore, his engagement could be labelled as *observer-as-participant* (Mulhall, 2003). Observations were conducted in a number of different occasions, including a welcoming event for a delegation of 40 members of the Terengganu Deaf community, the International Deaf Days organised by PDA and MFD, and by the YMCA Deaf Club, visits to local schools, and an event at the Parliament of Malaysia with 300 deaf people from all over the country.

A large number of rich descriptive written and audio field-notes were collected during and after the observations. Field-notes are a useful tool in qualitative inquiry, and they serve a double function: they allow researchers to record everything they see and hear during their investigation, but they also provide a means for critical reflection on the data during the process of collection (Bogdan & Biklen, 2007). As several authors point out, far from being comprehensive and objective depictions of the social world, field-notes are rather produced, constructed, and interpreted by researchers (Atkinson, 1992; Mulhall, 2003).

Ethical principles were respected throughout the whole research process. Participants were informed about the aims and the methodology of the study, gave their permission to record the interviews, and signed a consent form. A certified sign language interpreter was present during the whole process to guarantee mutual understanding and facilitate communication. In relation to the researcher's role and its ethical implications, we acknowledged that being a hearing, white, Italian, male, secular humanist researcher affiliated to European Universities, conducting a study in the Penang Deaf community could have raised questions of cultural legitimacy. However, previous experiences of the first author in multicultural contexts, several years of work and volunteer experience with deaf individuals in four countries, and a sound knowledge of deafness and the Deaf-World helped bridge the cultural gap. Additionally, the researcher's genuine commitment to learn the local sign language, and his full immersion in the Deaf community were truly appreciated by the locals, thus reducing distances and barriers.

2.3.3 Data Analysis and Discussion of Findings

All interviews were fully transcribed employing *clean transcripts* (Elliott, 2005), focusing on contents, and omitting considerations related to form, language, and structure of the narratives. These clean transcripts include spoken questions of the interviewer and spoken utterances of the interpreter, who translated participants' answers from BIM to English. At this stage, participants' names were substituted with pseudonyms and all other identifiable information was removed from the transcripts.

After several reviews of transcripts, written and audio field-notes, the interviews were coded adopting an inductive procedure: rather than selecting pre-determined categories, all segments describing specific phenomena were highlighted and organised in simple categories (Coffey & Atkinson, 1996). Through this process, 160 codes were identified and grouped in 10 code families. Subsequently, the 10 code families were cross-checked with the profile of each participant. Field-notes were not coded according to a standardised procedure; rather, the most relevant passages were highlighted and consulted throughout the whole analytical process. This procedure finally led to the elaboration of participants' thick descriptions (Geertz, 1973).

Participant one, Zara is a 30-year-old woman born in Sandakan, in the Malaysian state of Sabah, and her family has a mixed background from Europe and the Philippines. She was born deaf, but still has some residual hearing and uses hearing aids. She is the only deaf member of her family and her adolescence was profoundly marked by frequent relocations, limited communication, and experiences of discrimination. Zara is Christian and works as a teacher in a rehabilitation centre. She has been married for five years to a Chinese Deaf man, and they have a young deaf daughter.

Participant two, Ana is an ethnic Chinese 26-year-old woman born in Penang. She became deaf at the age of two, but still has some residual hearing and uses two hearing aids. Ana is the only deaf member of her family and proudly knows four languages: Hokkien (the Chinese dialect of Penang), Malaysian, English, and BIM. Ana is one of the few deaf people who started a business in Penang, related to graphic design and printing. Ana was born in a Chinese Buddhist family, but converted to Christianity at an early age.

Participant three, Amita is a 31-year-old ethnic Indian woman born in Kelantan. She became deaf at the age of seven: she is profoundly deaf in her left ear, but still has some residual hearing in the right one, and uses a hearing aid. Amita knows English, Malaysian, and BIM, but she never learned Tamil, the language spoken in her family, where she was the only deaf person. Amita works as coordinator at a rehabilitation centre, is married and has a two and a half year-old hearing daughter. Both Amita and her husband are Hindus.

Participant four, Farhad is a 25-year-old ethnic Malay man. He was born in England, but his family moved back to Johor Bahru before he was 2-years-old. He was born hearing, but he does not know with certainty the reason of his deafness and when it was diagnosed; he has some residual hearing in his left ear, and uses a hearing aid. Farhad is the only deaf person in his family, and both Malay culture and Islam are important to him. Farhad currently studies at a university, where he is the only deaf student.

Thematic analysis was performed triangulating codes, thick descriptions, and field-notes: this process was fundamental to examine emerging data in relation to the focus of the research, i.e. the exploration of participants' processes of identity development. Consequently, seven themes, were identified, and are presented below.

Theme 1: Impact of Communication on Identity
Communication naturally represents a transversal theme: deaf people's experiences within different social contexts are deeply influenced by access to communication. The concept of mother tongue is closely related to the process of identity development: while deaf oralists consider spoken language as their native tongue, people belonging to Deaf communities regard sign language as their mother tongue, and the local spoken language as a *foreign language* acquisition (Glickman, 1996; Ladd, 2003; Leeson, 2006; De Santis, 2010). All participants from this study considered BIM as their native language. This is consistent with data from previous research: cochlear implants are rare in Malaysia, and most deaf individuals prefer sign language to oral approaches (Umat et al., 2010; Lim, 2011). Moreover, all participants were multilingual and multicultural, as they could read and write in at least two languages, and had interactions with the hearing and Deaf worlds.

A number of studies underline the importance of bilingualism in the education of deaf children (Nikolaraizi & Hadjikakou, 2006; Grosjean, 2010; Swanwick, 2010; McIlroy & Storbeck, 2011): rather than being conceived as a passive acquisition of a second language, bilingualism should be endorsed as a best practice to raise and educate deaf children as bicultural individuals concurrently belonging to the Deaf and hearing worlds. Several authors further stress the importance of safeguarding the right to sign language, considered as a major prerequisite for Deaf people to communicate and develop their identities (Lane, 1992; Ladd, 2003; Leeson, 2006; Trovato, 2013). BIM is officially recognised in Malaysia (Government of Malaysia, 2008). Nonetheless, the existence of language barriers for deaf people emerged as a recurrent issue in this study:

So much is not fair for deaf people here. Like college or universities, there is no interpreter provided. Also hospital, police, they don't have an interpreter. Also in the TV very few times there is sign language interpreter, and we cannot watch. [...] And then about hotels, telephones... Communication... There is discrimination. (Ana)

The importance of sign language was a recurrent argument in all interviews, but was epitomised by Amita: she spent 15 years facing enormous communication barriers, had no friends, and felt lonely. She then joined a Deaf School, learnt sign language in a month, and started to communicate with everyone.

Theme 2: Impact of Deafness on Identity

All participants in this study were deaf, had some residual hearing, and used one or two hearing aids. Overall, deafness emerged as the most prevailing element shaping the identities of the participants in this study. They all learnt sign language when they entered Deaf school, considered BIM their native language, and were active in the Deaf community:

My first language is Malaysian Sign Language. (Zara)

Amita and Farhad demonstrated a strong attachment to Deaf culture, while Zara showed some uncertainty about it. Ana completely ignored the notion of Deaf culture, and clearly stated that in her opinion Deaf and hearing cultures are not separate:

For me... Deaf and hearing are not separate, also their culture is not separate... They are the same. They can go together, it is the same. (Ana)

On this point, Lim et al. (2006) underline that the current education system in Malaysia 'does not include Deaf culture as part of the syllabus for the Deaf' (p. vii): the majority of hearing people in the country, and surprisingly even some Deaf people, are unaware of the existence of Deaf culture.

Theme 3: Impact of Ethnicity on Identity

Ethnicity was the second sampling parameter in our research. While most participants mentioned the importance of ethnicity in their lives, ethnicity never emerged as a pivotal element of identity development.

Ana, Amita, and Farhad belonged to *large minorities*: Malay, Chinese, Indian. Zara belonged to a *small minority*, and defined herself as Sabahn.

Zara mentioned that people usually think that she is Chinese, due to the lineaments of her face: this shows that ethnic identity is not always immediately evident. Nevertheless, it is fair to say that individuals belonging to the three major ethnic groups are easily recognisable in Penang, both because of their physical traits and their clothes. For example, the vast majority of Malay women in Penang, including teachers, students, my interpreter, and all deaf Malay women wear the *hijab*, a scarf that covers head and chest. Many elder Indians wear traditional garments, but younger people (including Amita) use them as well. Most Chinese, instead, wear modern and casual clothes (including Ana). Additionally, people belonging to different ethnic groups tend to live and manage commercial activities in separate areas; certain neighbourhoods of George Town, as well as of other cities, are completely segregated, such as Little India and Chinatown. Nevertheless, individuals of different ethnic groups seem to live in harmony, without major conflicts or tension.

Most participants emphasised their ethnic belonging, their language, and underlined their attachment to the traditions of their families. However they expressed different feelings related to the impact of ethnicity on their individual identities. Zara clearly stated that ethnicity was not a relevant factor in her life:

I think ethnicity is not really important for me. (Zara)

Ana learnt Hokkien, the Chinese dialect used in Penang, and repeatedly defined herself as Chinese; however, she never mentioned Chinese traditions, and ethnicity did not emerge from her narrative as an extremely relevant factor in shaping her identity, both at individual and social levels. When asked to think about the most important factors defining her identity, Amita said Indian; however, she never specifically referred to ethnic Indian traditions during the interview. Farhad mentioned that he started to learn about Malay culture through his parents, but did not feel extremely knowledgeable about it; nevertheless, he clearly stated that ethnicity is a fundamental aspect of his identity:

Both cultures are important for me... I must be close to my family and follow the Malay culture... But at the same time I am in the Deaf Culture, and I spend time with them... (Farhad)

As discussed in the literature review, several studies highlight the impact of ethnic discrimination and racism on identity development in deaf individuals belonging to ethnic minorities (Aramburo, 1989; Anderson & Grace, 1991; Woll & Ladd, 2010; Ahmad et al., 2002; Atkin et al., 2002; Anderson & Miller, 2004; James & Woll, 2004; Smiler & McKee, 2007; Davis & McKay-Cody, 2010), but this did not emerge from this study. All participants encountered prejudice and discrimination throughout their lives. However, this was always related to their deafness, and they never felt discriminated because of their ethnicity. Even Zara, who was the only participant belonging to a *small minority*, stated that she never felt discriminated because of her ethnicity, even though she never had schoolmates or colleagues with the same ethnic background.

Theme 4: Impact of Religion on Identity
The impact of religion on individual and social identities clearly emerged in this study, both during interviews and observations. All participants highlighted their religious commitment and the importance of religion in their lives; nevertheless, participants also showed limited understanding of doctrines and religious traditions.

Farhad frequently highlighted the importance of Islam and of being a good Muslim; however, in the interview he demonstrated some confusion about ethnicity and religion, stating that Islam and Malay ethnicity are separated, that not all Malays are Muslims, and that they can be Christians or Buddhists. It is true that people belonging to other ethnic groups, such as Chinese and Indians, can be Muslim; however, Article 160 of the FCM (2010) clearly states that Malays are automatically Muslim, and it is illegal for them to change religion (Hamid & Azman, 2007). Farhad further underlined the need to create awareness programmes for deaf Muslims, and stated that the Muslim community should give more support to deaf people.

Amita never referred to Indian traditions; however, she often discussed about the importance of Hinduism in her life. She stated that she followed the tradition of her family, and that they would not have granted their approval for a marriage with a non-Hindu man. Amita further highlighted the struggles of deaf people to access Hindu culture. She started learning about it through her parents, although she encountered severe communication barriers in her family during childhood. She later improved her knowledge with the help of her husband and mother-in-law; in turn she tried to help deaf Hindu friends to learn more about Hindu traditions and rituals.

Zara and Ana were both Christians, and were the two participants who expressed the strongest religious commitment. Only a minority of people in Penang are Christians; nevertheless, on the island there are two Deaf churches, where celebrations are held completely in sign language, and three hearing churches offering sign language interpretations. None of these services are available to Muslims, Hindus, Buddhists, and followers of other religions, and this was highlighted by Farhad. As he pointed out, deaf Muslims often encounter several obstacles in accessing religion: for instance, there is no mosque providing sign language interpretation in Penang. Many of Farhad's deaf Muslim friends have poor knowledge about Islam, and do not like to fast. This can be socially perilous in Malaysia, where being a good Muslim (e.g. praying five times a day, going to the mosque, observing Ramadan, etc.) is a social imperative for Malays:

> Muslim culture is important... But some deaf friends have poor knowledge about Islam... So what happens is that they don't like to pray, they don't like to fast... This is really dangerous for the daily activities... So it would be important to develop awareness programmes about Islam for deaf Muslims... (Farhad)

The abundance of services for Deaf Christians is not entirely surprising: Christianity has a long tradition of evangelism and missionary work for deaf people (see, for instance, Kiyaga & Moores, 2003), and Zara's church is part of a larger Protestant Evangelical congregation originally founded in Seoul in 1982. Previous research documented the existence of a Roman Catholic Deaf community in Britain, separated from the main Deaf community (Woll & Ladd, 2010). Deaf Christians in Penang spend a considerable amount of time together, share a strong sense of connectivity, and have their own independent organisations, such as Deaf churches, and the YMCA Deaf Club (although deaf non-Christians are welcome to participate in its activities). Arguably, these might constitute the basis for the existence of a Deaf Christian sub-community, within the main Deaf community. Further research is required to evaluate this hypothesis.

Theme 5: Impact of Family on Identity
All participants were born from hearing parents, and were the only deaf members of their families. None of their parents ever learnt sign language. Three of the participants learnt the oral language used in their household to communicate with relatives, relying on lip-reading, residual hearing, and simple signs. Amita, however, never learnt Tamil, her parents' native

language, while Ana's parents adopted *normalisation strategies* (Atkin et al., 2002): initially, they did not allow her to use sign language, as they considered fundamental for her to learn to speak:

> I saw so many deaf there, using sign language. But my parents did not allow me to use sign language! My parents said "You must speak. When you are using sign language you also must speak". (Ana)

All participants wished their parents could sign, and most of them recounted experiences of isolation, loneliness, and boredom at home. This seems consistent with previous research (Ahmad et al., 2002; Atkin et al., 2002; Anderson & Miller, 2004; James & Woll, 2004; Smiler & McKee, 2007) showing that the lack of a common language is a recurrent factor with significant consequences for children's relationship with their parents in ethnic minority households.

According to the participants' narratives, parents did not demonstrate any knowledge of Deaf culture, and often ignored the existence of Deaf schools. Furthermore, the inability of parents to communicate with their deaf children affected their ability to share cultural and religious traditions. Nevertheless, all participants demonstrated high respect for members of their families, and Farhad stated that his parents are his role models and he seemed to justify them for never learning sign language:

> I would like it if some of them could sign... But it would be difficult to ask them to learn sign language... I don't want to force them. If they want to talk with me I ask them to use loud voice and to talk slowly. And sometimes I regret that I never taught them some sign language... (Farhad)

These displays of respect are not surprising, and appear to be rooted within the Malaysian culture, where seniority and authority are fundamental values (Razak, 2005), and 'the needs of the family have higher priority than the needs of its individual members' (Hegemann, 2008: p. 72).

Theme 6: Impact of Education on Identity

All the participants of this study attended hearing and Deaf schools where students of different ethnic backgrounds were mixed together. During participant observations in educational institutions in Penang, multicultural environments were always observed, as Malays, Chinese, Indians, as well as students from *small minorities*, were always mixed together in the same classroom. The segregation of some Malaysian hearing schools along ethnic parameters, discussed in the first section of this chapter, is not motivated by ethnicity *per se*: rather, the goal is the adoption of a different language, such as Tamil or Chinese, as medium for instruction. This easily explains the absence of ethnically segregated Deaf schools, where BIM is the primary language used by deaf students, and KTBM is the main medium of instruction.

Consistent with findings of previous studies (Lane et al., 1996, Jarvis, 2007; Glaser & van Pletzen, 2012; Marschark et al., 2012; Miles, Wapling, & Beart, 2011; Schley et al., 2011), participants' narratives highlighted frequent negative experiences in hearing educational and work environments, stressing the lack of appropriate support and resources for deaf individuals. Conversely, all participants had positive experiences in Deaf schools, were they learnt BIM and discovered the Deaf community. Two participants, Amita and Farhad, attended a hearing primary school, and in both cases were included in multicultural classes. Farhad is Malay and had no need to be sent to segregated schools to learn Malaysian. Amita, however, is Indian, and her parents could have sent her to a Tamil vernacular school. Given the enormous communication problems that she faced during childhood, it may be speculated that they decided to send her to a standard school to avoid further difficulties.

Both Amita and Farhad recounted experiences of isolation and discrimination in hearing schools in relation to their deafness: they never received appropriate support, and they felt abandoned and segregated:

> My teacher could not accept me... Then my parents told me to stop kindergarten, and my mom took the responsibility to teach me how to speak. Then at seven I went to a hearing school. [...] I had communication problems, hearing problems. My school didn't know details about me, so when I entered the school they put me to seat at the end of the class... And I couldn't hear anything when my teacher was teaching. (Amita)

All participants, however, eventually entered Deaf schools, where they learnt BIM, made new friends, and had positive experiences. Deaf schools were also pivotal in introducing most of the participants to Deaf organisations and the Deaf community.

Three participants spent at least one year at the FSD in Penang; Zara and Amita even moved from other States to study there. When this study was conducted, there were 3 students enrolled in a pre-primary class, 37 in primary school, and 134 in secondary school at the FSD. Students, teachers, and members of the administration belong to various ethnic groups. Nakamura (2002), however, noted that since the opening of FSD all principals have been ethnic Chinese: this tradition did not change, as the head teachers are Chinese both in the primary and secondary school. Additionally, two highly surprising things were observed during our visit at FSD: in the primary school there were only two deaf teachers, and also at secondary level only two out of 52 teachers were deaf. It is not surprising therefore that both deaf teachers and students lamented communication problems with hearing teachers.

All participants attended college and studied in multi-ethnic classes, and lack of support emerged as a recurrent theme in hearing environments. Zara an Amita attended Deaf courses, while Ana and Farhad were integrated in hearing classes. Ana lamented the complete lack of support from the college; Farhad was entitled for a period to a sign language interpreter, but maintained that more support is needed. Farhad is the only participant who continued his studies after college, entering a graphic communication course at university. He is the only deaf student there, and complained about the lack of adequate support:

> Since I have started I didn't receive support from any interpreter. I am trying to study hard, but I have failed two subjects... [...] I think that the government or Deaf organisations should do something to support deaf students in the university... (Farhad)

Previous literature suggests that schools often lack cultural sensitivity in relation to ethnic minorities, and deaf children of ethnic minority backgrounds experience discrimination and racism (Aramburo, 1989; Anderson & Grace, 1991; Woll & Ladd, 2010; Ahmad et al., 2002; Atkin et al., 2002; Anderson & Miller, 2004; James & Woll, 2004; Smiler & McKee, 2007; Davis & McKay-Cody, 2010). However, it is noteworthy that participants in this study always described multicultural educational environments and never felt discriminated because of their ethnicity:

> In both schools they had different ethnic groups... All together! (Amita)

Theme 7: Impact of Employment on Identity
All participants had work experiences in hearing companies. Both Zara and Amita shared experiences of isolation and discrimination in hearing companies: they rarely received support from employers and colleagues. Amita, however, narrated her positive experience in the human resources department of a supermarket:

> I got the job at the human resource department. [...] my boss saw me working and said "You are very confident, you can do it. You are deaf, but you still can do a good job". I loved that, I was really thankful. (Amita)

In terms of ethnicity, except for Amita who worked for a period in a company where she was the only Indian, in all other circumstances, participants described multi-ethnic work environments, and never reported experiences of discrimination related to their ethnic backgrounds. Experiences of discrimination in employment, therefore, appeared to be related only to deafness, and not to ethnicity.

Article 23 of the Universal Declaration of Human Rights (United Nations, 1948) and Article 27 of the CRPD (United Nations, 2006) clearly remark the right of each individual to gain access to inclusive and accessible work environments. According to the Social Welfare Department (2009), there were 35,368 deaf and hearing impaired people employed in Malaysia in 2009. Many deaf individuals, however, only have access to vocational trainings and are employed in sectors such as air-conditioning, plumbing, electrical repair, dressmaking, and graphic design (Jaafar & Mee, 2010). Limited educational opportunities result in reduced employability: as a consequence, deaf individuals have fewer opportunities to become economically independent, conduct satisfactory lives, and mature positive and successful constructions of identity (Lane et al., 1996).

2.4   CONCLUSIONS AND RECOMMENDATIONS

Research conducted in different countries has demonstrated that experiences within family, education, employment, and other social environments have a critical impact on self-perception, identity development, and social inclusion of deaf people belonging to minority ethnic groups (Ahmad et al., 2002; Anderson & Grace, 1991; Aramburo, 1989; Atkin et al., 2002; Foster & Kinuthia, 2003; James & Woll, 2004; Smiler &

McKee, 2007; Davis & McKay-Cody, 2010; Woll & Ladd, 2010). The study presented in this chapter is the first research exploring the interplay between deafness and ethnicity ever conducted in Malaysia. The aim of the research was to collect narratives of deaf individuals belonging to different ethnic groups and to explore in some depth their processes of identity development.

Three participants affirmed the importance of ethnicity and deafness in defining their present identity, and highlighted their belonging to the ethnic and Deaf communities; only one of them clearly stated that ethnicity was not a relevant factor in her life. However, participants' narratives mainly revolved around deafness and communication, and ethnicity never emerged as a pivotal element of identity development from their accounts. All participants were active members of the Deaf community. Participants who expressed the importance of ethnicity for their identity, did not mention any involvement in specific activities of their ethnic community. The participant who did not consider ethnicity important, had no contact with people of the same ethnic background. Literature demonstrates the existence in several countries of Deaf ethnic sub-communities, separated from the main Deaf community (Aramburo, 1989; Woll & Ladd, 2010; James & Woll, 2004). This seems not to be the case in Malaysia: while separations are present in the hearing society, the Deaf community does not appear to be fragmented along ethnic boundaries. Arguably, elements were collected that may allow us to speculate on the existence of a Deaf Christian sub-community.

Hence, deafness clearly emerged from this research as the most relevant element in shaping participants' individual and social identities. All participants considered BIM as their first language, but none of their hearing parents ever learned it. This had two consequences: on the one hand, parents had difficulties in communicating and sharing ethnic and cultural traditions with their children; on the other hand, participants developed limited knowledge of their own cultural heritage, and frequently experienced isolation. For these reasons, we recommend that parents and siblings of deaf children in Malaysia are encouraged and supported to learn sign language, discover Deaf culture, and participate in the Deaf community.

Furthermore, participants always described multicultural educational environments and never felt discriminated because of their ethnicity. Conversely, episodes of discrimination and exclusion were frequently reported in hearing schools in relation to their deafness, along with the lack of support from the educational institutions at all levels. Most participants shared positive experiences in Deaf schools, but the employment of deaf teachers in these settings is still extremely limited: this may be detrimental, as students encounter communication barriers with hearing teachers, and lack adult deaf role models. More research is needed to evaluate achievements and challenges of integration programmes for deaf students in hearing classrooms. It would be worthwhile to conduct further research also within Deaf schools, to address issues related to Deaf role models and the paucity of Deaf teachers. It is fair to say that more efforts are required from educational and governmental institutions to ensure equitable access to education for deaf individuals, particularly at college and university level. Additional research is also required to explore access to employment for deaf people in Malaysia. Arguably, more training programmes for deaf teachers should be implemented, to promote their involvement in the education of deaf students, reinforce Deaf culture, and create new employment opportunities.

The impact of religion on individual and social identities clearly emerged from the study, as all participants demonstrated a strong religious commitment. Nevertheless, while Deaf Christians living in Penang have access to a wide range of facilities and services, it seems to be the case that more support is required for deaf Muslims, Hindus, Buddhists, and followers of other religions, as they encounter relevant communication barriers, hindering their access to celebrations and doctrines.

Consistent with previous studies (Ahmad et al., 2002; Anderson & Grace, 1991; Aramburo, 1989; Atkin et al., 2002; Foster & Kinuthia, 2003; Anderson & Miller, 2004; James & Woll, 2004; Smiler & McKee, 2007; Davis & McKay-Cody, 2010; Woll & Ladd, 2010), both experiences of discrimination and belonging within family, school, work, religious and social environments played a fundamental role in shaping individual identities of the participants. All participants were multilingual: besides BIM, each of them knew two or three other languages, such as Malaysian, Hokkien, and English. Participants could also be defined as multicultural: they had interactions in the Deaf and hearing worlds, and expressed attachments to their ethnic and religious communities. One participant offered a clear example of multiculturalism: she was deaf, Chinese, a fervent Christian, a successful entrepreneur, a member of the Deaf community, and an active participant in the hearing society.

Finally, in line with previous research (Ahmad et al., 2002; Foster & Kinuthia, 2003; James & Woll, 2004; Smiler & McKee, 2007; Davis & McKay-Cody, 2010), participants from this study did not conceive identity as a static attribute, rejected notions of primacy between different attributes, and never defined themselves just as deaf, or in relation to their ethnicity. Instead, different elements seemed to contribute to participants' own self-perception, including deafness, ethnicity, religion, language, age and profession, and their identities above all appeared to be fluid and contextual.

REFERENCES

Abdullah, M. N. L. Y. (2013). Embracing diversity by bridging the school-to-work transition of students with disabilities in Malaysia. In G. Tchibozo (Ed.), *Cultural and social diversity and the transition from education to work* (pp. 163–184). Dordrecht, Heidelberg, London and New York: Springer.

Ahmad, W. I. U., Atkin, K., & Farhades, L. (2002). Being deaf and being other things: Young Asian people negotiating identities. *Social Science & Medicine, 55*(10), 1757–1769.

Ahmad, W. I. U., Darr, A., Farhades, L., & Nisar, G. (1998). *Deafness and ethnicity*. Bristol: Policy Press.

Airriess, C. A. (2000). Malaysia and Brunei. In T. R. Leinbach & R. Ulack (Eds.), *Southeast Asia: Diversity and development*. Upper Saddle River, NJ: Prentice Hall.

Ali, M. M., Mustapha, R., & Jelas, Z. M. (2006). An empirical study on teachers' perceptions towards inclusive education in Malaysia. *International Journal of Special Education, 21*(3), 36–44.

Anderson, G. B., & Grace, C. A. (1991). Black deaf adolescents: A diverse and underserved population. *The Volta Review, 93*(5), 73–86. Reprinted in Fuller, J. B.

Anderson, G. B., & Miller, K. R. (2004). In their own words: Researching stories about the lives of deaf people of color. *Multicultural Perspectives, 6*(2), 28–33.

Aramburo, A. J. (1989). Sociolinguistic aspects of the black deaf community. In C. Lucas (Ed.), *The Sociolinguistics of the deaf community* (pp. 103–119). San Diego: Academic Press Inc.

Atkin, K., Ahmad, W. I., & Farhades, L. (2002). Young South Asian deaf people and their families: Negotiating relationships and identities. *Sociology of Health & Illness, 24*(1), 21–45.

Atkinson, P. (1992). *Understanding ethnographic texts*. Newbury Park: Sage Publications.

Berger, P. L., & Luckmann, T. (1971). *The social construction of reality: A treatise in the sociology of knowledge.* Reprint, Harmondsworth, Middlesex: Penguin Books (first published: 1966).

Blumer, H. (1969). *Symbolic interactionism: Perspective and method.* Englewood Cliffs: Prentice-Hall.

Bogdan, R. C., & Biklen, S. K. (2007). *Qualitative research for education: An introduction to theories and methods* (5th ed.). New York: Pearson Education Group.

Bryman, A. (2012). *Social research methods* (4th ed.). Oxford: Oxford University Press.

Byrne, B. (2012). Qualitative interviewing. In C. Seale (Ed.), *Researching society and culture* (3rd ed.). London: Sage Publications.

Byrne, M. R. (1998). Diversity within the deaf or hard of hearing population: Wisdom from seeing the whole. *Early Child Development and Care, 147*(1), 55–70.

Central Intelligence Agency. (2009). *The World Fact Book: Malaysia.* Retrieved May 10, 2017, from https://www.cia.gov/library/publications/the-world-factbook/geos/my.html

Chandra, K. (2006). What is ethnic identity and does it matter? *Annual Review of Political Science, 9,* 397–424.

Chua, A. (2004). *World on fire: How exporting free market democracy breeds ethnic hatred and global instability.* New York: Anchor.

Clark, M., Brown, R., & Karrapaya, R. (2012). An initial look at the quality of life of Malaysian families that include children with disabilities. *Journal of Intellectual Disability Research, 56*(1), 45–60.

Coffey, A., & Atkinson, P. (1996). *Making sense of qualitative data: Complementary research strategies.* Thousand Oaks, CA: Sage Publications.

Cohen, L., Manion, L., & Morrison, K. (2007). *Research methods in education* (6th ed.). New York: Routledge.

Davis, J., & McKay-Cody, M. (2010). Signed languages and American Indian communities: Considerations for interpreting work and research. In R. McKee & J. Davis (Eds.), *Sign language interpreting in multilingual and multicultural contexts* (pp. 119–157). Washington, DC: Gallaudet University Press.

De Santis, D. (2010). Lo sviluppo del linguaggio nel bambino sordo e udente: due modalità comunicative a confronto [Language development in deaf and hearing children: A comparison between two communication modalities]. *Studi di Glottodidattica* [*Studies in Glottodidactics*], 4(1), 75–91.

Edwards, R., & Ribbens, J. (1998). Living on the edges: Public knowledge, private lives, personal experience. In J. Ribben & R. Edwards (Eds.), *Feminist dilemmas in qualitative research* (pp. 1–24). London: Sage Publications.

Elliott, J. (2005). *Using narrative in social research. Qualitative and quantitative approaches.* London: Sage Publications.

Erting, C., & Woodward, J. (1979). Sign language and the deaf community a sociolinguistic profile. *Discourse Processes, 2*(4), 283–300.

Ethnologue. (2013). *Malaysian Sign Language.* Retrieved May 10, 2017, from http://www.ethnologue.com/language/xml

Federal Constitution of Malaysia (FCM). (2010). Retrieved May 10, 2017, from http://www.agc.gov.my/agcportal/uploads/files/Publications/FC/Federal%20Consti%20(BI%20text).pdf

Foster, S., & Kinuthia, W. (2003). Deaf persons of Asian American, Hispanic American, and African-American backgrounds: A study of intra-individual diversity and identity. *Journal of Deaf Studies and Deaf Education, 8*(3), 271–290.

Geertz, C. (1973). *The interpretation of cultures.* New York: Basic Books.

Ghadim, N. A., Alias, N., Rashid, S. M. M., & Yusoff, M. Y. Z. B. M. (2013). Mother's perspective toward al-Quran education for hearing impaired children in Malaysia. *The Malaysian Online Journal of Educational Technology, 1*(4), 26–30.

Glaser, M., & van Pletzen, E. (2012). Inclusive education for Deaf students: Literacy practices and South African sign language. *Southern African Linguistics and Applied Language Studies, 30*(1), 25–37.

Glickman, N. D. (1996). The development of culturally Deaf identities. In N. S. Glickman & M. A. Harvey (Eds.), *Culturally affirmative psychotherapy with Deaf persons* (pp. 115–153). Mahway, NJ: Lawrence Erlbaum Associates.

Goodley, D., & Lawthom, R. (2011). Disability, community and empire: Indigenous psychologies and social psychoanalytic possibilities. *International Journal of Inclusive Education, 15*(1), 101–115.

Government of Malaysia. (1996). *Education Act 1996.* Retrieved May 10, 2017, from http://planipolis.iiep.unesco.org/sites/planipolis/files/ressources/malaysia_education_act_1996.pdf

Government of Malaysia. (2008). *Persons with Disabilities Act 2008.* Retrieved May 10, 2017, from http://www.ilo.org/dyn/natlex/docs/ELECTRONIC/86297/117930/F139356912/MYS86297.pdf

Gray, D. E. (2014). *Doing research in the real world* (3rd ed.). London: Sage.

Grosjean, F. (2010). Bilingualism, biculturalism, and deafness. *International Journal of Bilingual Education and Bilingualism, 13*(2), 133–145.

Hamid, J., & Azman, S. (2007, May 30). Malaysia's Lina Joy loses Islam conversion case. *Reuters,* Retrieved May 10, 2017, from http://www.reuters.com/article/2007/05/30/us-malaysia-religion-ruling-idUSSP20856820070530

Hartas, D. (2010). The epistemological context of quantitative and qualitative research. In D. Hartas (Ed.), *Educational research and inquiry: Qualitative and quantitative approaches* (pp. 33–53). New York: Continuum International Publishing Group.

Hegemann, R. (2008). Explaining the potential for conflict: Malaysia between tradition and modernity. *ASIEN, 109,* 65–77.

Hirschman, C. (1987). The meaning and measurement of ethnicity in Malaysia: An analysis of census classifications. *Journal of Asian Studies, 46*(3), 555–582.

Horowitz, D. (1985). *Ethnic groups in conflict.* Berkeley, CA: University Press.

Humphries, T., Kushalnagar, P., Mathur, G., Napoli, D. J., Padden, C., Rathmann, C., et al. (2012). Language acquisition for deaf children: Reducing the harms of zero tolerance to the use of alternative approaches. *Harm Reduction Journal, 9*(16). https://doi.org/10.1186/1477-7517-9-16

Hurlbut, H. M. (2000). A preliminary survey of the signed languages of Malaysia. In *Cross-linguistic perspectives in sign language research* (pp. 31–44). Gallaudet University Press.

Jaafar, J. M., & Mee, M. Y. (2010). Learning from the Deaf to enhance learning for the Deaf". *The Open Rehabilitation Journal, 3,* 16–22.

James, M., & Woll, B. (2004). Black Deaf or Deaf black? Being black and Deaf in Britain. In A. Pavlenko & A. Blackledge (Eds.), *Negotiation of identities in multilingual contexts* (pp. 125–160). Clevedon: Multilingual Matters.

Jarvis, J. (2007). Exclusion by inclusion? Issues for deaf pupils and their mainstream teachers. *Education 3–13: International Journal of Primary, Elementary and Early Years Education, 30*(2), 47–51.

Jenkins, R. (2014). *Social identity* (4th ed.). Oxon: Routledge.

Kirk, S., Gallagher, J., Coleman, M. R., & Anastasiow, N. J. (2011). *Educating exceptional children* (13th ed.). Wadsworth. Cengage Learning.

Kiyaga, N. B., & Moores, D. F. (2003). Deafness in Sub-Saharan Africa. *American Annals of the Deaf, 148*(1), 18–24.

Ladd, P. (2003). *Understanding deaf culture: In search of deafhood.* Clevedon: Multilingual Matters.

Ladd, P., & Lane, H. (2013). Deaf ethnicity, deafhood, and their relationship. *Sign Language Studies, 13*(4), 565–579.

Lane, H. (1992). *The mask of benevolence: Disabling the deaf community.* New York: Alfred A. Knopf.

Lane, H., Hoffmeister, R., & Bahan, B. (1996). *A journey into the Deaf world.* San Diego, CA: DawnSignPress.

Leeson, L. (2006). *Signed languages in education in Europe—A preliminary exploration. (Preliminary study. Languages of education).* Strasbourg: Council of Europe Language Policy Division.

Leigh, I. W. (2009). *A lens on deaf identities: Perspectives on deafness.* New York, NY: Oxford University Press.

Lim, L., Woo, S., & Chong, A. (2006). *Understanding deaf culture: Malaysian perspectives.* Kuala Lumpur: Majudiri Y Foundation for the Deaf.

Lim, R. (2011, June 3). Govt may provide free cochlear implants for children of poor families. *The Star Online,* Retrieved May 10, 2017, from http://www.thestar.com.my/story/?file=%2f2011%2f6%2f3%2fnation%2f8828175

Lodico, M. G., Spaulding, D. T., & Voegtle, K. H. (2010). *Methods in educational research: From theory to practice* (2nd ed.). San Francisco, CA: Jossey-Bass.

Lyotard, J. F. (1984). *The post-modern condition: A report on knowledge.* Minneapolis, MN: University of Minnesota Press.

Malaysian Department of Statistics. (2016). *Current population estimates, Malaysia, 2014–2016.* Retrieved May 10, 2017, from https://www.dosm.gov.my/v1/index.php?r=column/ctheme&menu_id=L0pheU43NWJwRWVSZklWdzQ4TlhUUT09&bul_id=OWlxdEVoYlJCS0hUZzJyRUcvZEYxZz09

Marschark, M., Bull, R., Sapere, P., Nordmann, E., Skene, W., Lukomski, J., et al. (2012). Do you see what I see? School perspectives of deaf children, hearing children and their parents. *European Journal of Special Needs Education, 27*(4), 483–497.

Mascia, K., & Mascia, J. (2012). The bioethics of providing cochlear implants to children: Informed choices and autonomous decision-making. *Journal of the American Deafness & Rehabilitation Association (JADARA), 45*(2), 273–286.

Maxwell, J. A. (1996). *Qualitative research design: An interactive approach.* Thousand Oaks, CA: Sage.

McIlroy, G., & Storbeck, C. (2011). Development of deaf identity: An ethnographic study. *Journal of Deaf Studies and Deaf Education, 16*(4), 494–511.

Mead, G. H. (1934). *Mind, self, and society.* Chicago: University of Chicago Press.

Miles, S., Wapling, L., & Beart, J. (2011). Including deaf children in primary schools in Bushenyi, Uganda: A community-based initiative. *Third World Quarterly, 32*(8), 1515–1525.

Mulhall, A. (2003). In the field: Notes on observation in qualitative research. *Journal of Advanced Nursing, 41*(3), 306–313.

Murad, D. (2013, September 20). MFD: Massive shortage of sign language interpreters. *The Star Online,* Retrieve May 10, 2017, from http://www.thestar.com.my/News/Nation/2013/09/20/more-interpreters-needed/

Nakamura, K. (2002). Deafness, ethnicity, and minority politics in modern Malaysia. *Macalester International, 12,* Article 20.

Napier, J. (2002). The D/deaf–H/hearing debate. *Sign Language Studies, 2*(2), 141–149.

Nikolaraizi, M., & Hadjikakou, K. (2006). The role of educational experiences in the development of deaf identity. *Journal of Deaf Studies and Deaf Education, 11*(4), 477–492.

Razak, A. A. (2005). Behind the scene: The "culture" of interviewing in Malaysia. In A. P. Robinson-Pant (Ed.), *Cross-cultural perspectives on educational research* (pp. 85–88). Maidenhead: Open University Press.

Schley, S., Walter, G. G., Weathers, R. R., Hemmeter, J., Hennessey, J. C., & Burkhauser, R. V. (2011). Effect of postsecondary education on the economic status of persons who are deaf or hard of hearing. *Journal of Deaf Studies and Deaf Education, 16*(4), 524–536.

Scott-Hill, M. (2003). Deafness/Disability—Problematising notions of identity, culture and structure. In S. Ridell & N. Watson (Eds.), *Disability, culture and identity* (pp. 86–104). London: Pearson.

Smiler, K., & McKee, R. L. (2007). Perceptions of Māori deaf identity in New Zealand. *Journal of Deaf Studies and Deaf Education, 12*(1), 93–111.

Stebnicki, J. A. M., & Coeling, H. V. (1999). The culture of the deaf. *Journal of Transcultural Nursing, 10*(4), 350–357.

Stryker, S. (1968). Identity salience and role performance: The relevance of symbolic interaction theory for family research. *Journal of Marriage and Family, 30*(4), 558–564.

Sultana, F. (2007). Reflexivity, positionality and participatory ethics: Negotiating fieldwork dilemmas in international research. *ACME: An International E-Journal for Critical Geographies, 6*(3), 374–385.

Swanwick, R. (2010). Policy and practice in sign bilingual education: development, challenges and directions. *International Journal of Bilingual Education and Bilingualism, 13*(2), 147–158.

Trovato, S. (2013). A stronger reason for the right to sign languages. *Sign Language Studies, 13*(3), 401–422.

Umat, C., Siti, H. K., & Azlizawati, A. R. (2010). Auditory functionality and early use of speech in a group of pediatric cochlear implant users. *The Medical journal of Malaysia, 65*(1), 7–13.

UNESCO. (1994). *The salamanca statement and framework for action on special needs education: World conference on special needs education: Access and quality.* Salamanca: UNESCO.

United Nations. (1948). *Universal declaration of human rights.* Paris: UN.

United Nations. (2006). *Convention on the rights of persons with disabilities.* New York: UN.

Wah, L. L. (2010). Different strategies for embracing inclusive education: A snap shot of individual cases from three countries. *International Journal of Special Education, 25*(3), 98–109.

Woll, B., & Ladd, P. (2010). Deaf communities. In M. Marschark & P. E. Spencer (Eds.), *The Oxford handbook of deaf studies, language and education* (Vol. 2, pp. 159–172). Oxford: University Press.

Woodward, J. (1972). Implications for sociolinguistic research among the deaf. *Sign Language Studies, 1*, 1–7.

Wrigley, O. (1996). *The politics of deafness.* Washington, DC: Gallaudet University Press.

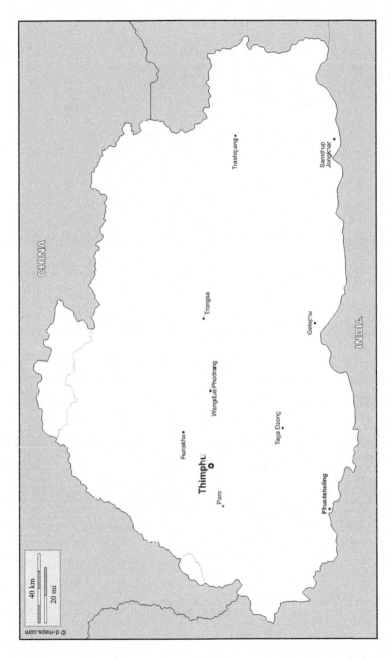

Fig. 3.1 Map of Bhutan (Source: http://www.d-maps.com/m/asia/bhoutan/bhoutan21.gif)

CHAPTER 3

The Conceptualisation of Inclusion and Disability in Bhutan

Dawa Dukpa and Leda Kamenopoulou

Abstract Chapter 3 presents a research that explored the concepts *Disability* and *Inclusion* from the perspective of Bhutanese people. There is scarce research on the education of children with disabilities in Bhutan. A qualitative research design was adopted and semi-structured interviews were conducted with 15 people. According to the findings, participants understood disability primarily as product of genetic inheritance, medical condition or accident. Some held negative views about the parents of disabled children, considering them somehow responsible for their children's disability, and some associated disability with karma (bad fate). Moreover, they held quite different views as to what inclusion means. The authors call for improved training programmes for teachers on inclusion and

NB: *Some of the data used for the research presented here was also used in a research focused on Bhutanese teachers' perspectives and published as a journal article.*

D. Dukpa (✉)
Royal University of Bhutan, Paro, Bhutan

L. Kamenopoulou
University of Roehampton, London, UK

L. Kamenopoulou (ed.), *Inclusive Education and Disability in the Global South*, https://doi.org/10.1007/978-3-319-72829-2_3

disability, as well as programmes to raise awareness in the wider population of Bhutan.

Keywords Inclusion • Disability • Perceptions • Semi-structured interviews • Bhutan

> *'I think some people are born disabled probably because of past karma or fate.'*
> *(Father of a disabled child)*

3.1   Introduction

Since the Salamanca Statement (UNESCO, 1994) many countries around the world have been increasingly moving towards the inclusion of children with disabilities in mainstream schools. Similarly, Bhutan has also embraced the notion of inclusive education according to its Ministry of Education (MoE, 2012). Several policy documents indicate that inclusion is an important priority in the Bhutanese education system (for example, MoE, 2012, 2014), as inclusive education values seem to influence education policy in Bhutan.

The study reported in this chapter was directed by one main question: *How are 'inclusion' and 'disability' perceived by the Bhutanese people?* We wanted to explore the concepts 'disability' and 'inclusion' as seen through the perspectives of people in Bhutan. There is very scarce research on the topics of disability and inclusion (Dorji, 2015; Gyamtsho & Maxwell, 2012; Kamenopoulou & Dukpa, 2017). The education of children with disabilities, and in particular their inclusion in mainstream schools remain understudied in the context of Bhutan. Therefore, we wanted to capture the concepts 'disability' and 'inclusion' that are contextually relevant to Bhutan. We conducted an interview based qualitative research, using semi-structured interviews to collect data. The sample comprised 6 teachers working with children with disabilities or who had experience of working in the field of inclusion and disability and 9 other professionals. The process of data analysis was driven by our research questions: 1. *What is 'inclusion' according to the Bhutanese people?* 2. *What is 'disability' according to the Bhutanese people?* 3. *How do Bhutanese people understand the relationship between 'disability' and 'inclusion'?* Accordingly, the results were grouped in 3 broad thematic areas: (i) Perception of inclusion (ii) Perception of disability (iii) Perception of relationship between the two concepts.

Findings revealed that participants understood disability primarily as product of genetic inheritance, medical condition or an accident. They moreover held quite negative views of the parents of disabled children, considering them somehow responsible for their children's disability due to lack of appropriate nutrition and bad habits of the pregnant mother. Some seemed to associate disability with past karma (bad fate). Moreover, the people interviewed broadly understood inclusion as placing children with disabilities in school alongside other children who are not identified as having disabilities. However, some participants understood inclusion as a human right and expressed the view that no one should be denied or deprived of that right. We argue that the findings from this research call for improved training programmes on inclusion and disability for teachers in Bhutan as well as programmes to increase disability awareness in the wider population.

3.2   The Bhutanese Context

Bhutan is a small Himalayan kingdom between China in the north and India in the south. Bhutan has a land area of 38,394 square kilometres and population of 733,004 as projected in 2013 (National Statistics Bureau, 2013). It is the only country in the world that has Gross National Happiness (GNH) as a constitutional aim (Ura & Galay, 2004). GNH emphasises the balanced integration of material development and psychological well-being (Ura & Galay, 2004). The principle of GNH states that every citizen of Bhutan, including disabled people, should enjoy equal rights in political, economic, cultural, social and other aspects of life (Dorji, 2015; Kamenopoulou & Dukpa, 2017). It is important to stress the concept of GNH here, because as rightly noted by Schuelka (2014, 2015), GNH is central to Bhutan's education strategy.

Bhutan became a democracy in 2008 when Druk Gyalpo (loosely translated as 'the dragon King') Jigme Singye Wangchuk, the fourth hereditary king of Bhutan handed over the power of governance to the Bhutanese people by introducing parliamentary democracy. Bhutan had remained isolated from the rest of the world until the early 1960s, when the first motor roads were constructed connecting Bhutan with India. Within the last five decades, Bhutan has made a steady move towards modernisation, witnessing change and progress in every aspect of development. Institutionalisation of schooling became an integral part of the nation's development. Schuelka (2013) remarks that prior to the 1960s, there were very few children who went to school and formal schooling was non-existent. He moreover stresses that 'the rise in prominence and participation of schooling in Bhutan in the last 50 years has been truly remarkable' (p. 7). In the span of five decades, Bhutan's education system has grown from a handful of schools to 504 public schools and 35 private schools, educating over 172,857 children (MoE, 2015). Phuntsho (2000) puts it in the following words:

> [O]f all the changes and development that the kingdom of Bhutan saw in the last half of the 20th century the ones in education are the most evident, momentous and far reaching. (p. 9)

Schuelka (2014, 2015) observes that the Bhutanese education system constantly tries to reconcile the traditional Buddhist-monastic education system, the British missionary and colonial education systems, and human rights informed education, based on modern student-centred approaches and inclusive education values. The result of having to reconcile and consider the different systems is that often, contradictory structures and systems are put in place (Schuelka, 2014, 2015). For example schools that are built in line with the traditional Buddhist monastic architecture often obstruct accessibility of wheelchairs. Similarly, the Buddhist monastic system and the colonial education system are mostly based on the expectation of rote learning from all, which can again be contradictory to a more inclusive system that acknowledges learners' diverse learning styles.

Amid these challenges, Bhutan is on a long-term mission to provide access to mainstream education for all children with disabilities. Bhutan's commitment to its children is evidenced by the country's decision to ratify the UN Convention on the Rights of the Child (CRC) in 1990 and sign the UN Convention on the Rights of Persons with Disabilities (UN, 2006) in 2010. The Royal Government of Bhutan strives to maintain and enhance an inclusive approach in order to improve access and meet the needs of those learners with disabilities. The 2015 Annual Education Statistics report states that:

> [T]he long-term objective of the Special Education Services Programme is to provide access to general education in regular schools for all children with

disabilities and special needs, including those with physical, mental and other types of impairment. (MoE, 2015: p. 32)

In 2016, The Ministry of Education in consultation with other stakeholders developed *The Standards for Inclusive Education*, which were endorsed by the annual education conference held in January 2017. The *Standards for Inclusive Education* is a tool to support schools in Bhutan towards becoming more inclusive (MoE, 2017), which is a huge step in the move towards inclusion. However, it should be noted that as of 2016, there are 10 mainstream schools with SEN programmes catering to 611 children with special educational needs and 2 specialised institutes catering to students who are deaf or blind (MoE, 2017). The Standards for Inclusive Education document states that the 10 mainstream schools that have been identified as being able to support students with disabilities should be referred to as 'schools with SEN programme' and not 'SEN schools'. It further states that SEN schools will only have children with disabilities and as such they are not fully inclusive. Moreover, the Draktsho Vocational Training Centre is an NGO that currently provides basic education and vocational skills training to about 116 children and youth with special needs in Bhutan (MoE, 2017).

Hence, despite Bhutan's rhetorical commitments to greater inclusion in education, in reality children with disabilities are still placed in segregated schools and other educational institutions catering to their needs.

3.3   Understanding 'Disability' and 'Inclusion'

3.3.1   *Disability*

According to Metts (2004), disability is a complex interconnected biomedical phenomenon that exists in all societies. It is a normal phenomenon that affects a predictable and identifiable sample of the population in all societies. The complexity of the concept of disability is evident in the existence of diverse local interpretations of the same concept depending on both the nature of impairment and the cultural context (Giffard-Lindsay, 2007).

When trying to construct an understanding of disability in a given context, it is important to highlight that the concept of disability has evolved over time and has undergone tremendous change in terms of how people think about its causes and development. Moreover, people have progressed in their attitude and behaviour towards persons with disabilities over the years. Prior to 1970s, disability was generally considered as a problem falling primarily under the responsibility of medical or rehabilitation professionals. Individuals with disabilities were often left to the professionals to be cured or rehabilitated (Ralston & Hoe, 2010). Disability was almost exclusively understood as a result of functional limitations and psychological loss in line with the dominant individual or medical approach to disability (Barnes, 2000).

The UN's declaration of the Rights of Mentally Retarded Persons in 1971 and the declaration of the Rights of Disabled Persons in 1975 followed by the designation of 1981 as the 'International Year of Disabled Persons' (IYDP) and 1983–92 the Decade of Disabled Persons' intensified the growing level of international interest and activism in disability issues and policies (Barnes & Mercer, 2005). Another important landmark in the international scene was the United Nations' 'Standard Rules on the Equalization of Opportunities for People with Disabilities' issued following the 1982 World Programme of Action Concerning Disabled Persons, a global strategy to enhance disability prevention, rehabilitation and equalisation of opportunities for people with disabilities (UN, 1993). These and other initiatives have been moving the idea of disability from an individual based, medical model perspective to the recognition of disability as being influenced by personal, social and environmental factors. This recognition came after the development of the International Classification of Impairments, Disabilities and Handicaps (ICIDH) by the World Health Organization (WHO) in 1980. More importantly, the ICIDH recognises the fact that policy has the power to alter environmental contexts such as cultures, institutions and the physical environments and thus increase the social and economic accessibility of people with disabilities (Metts, 2000). The ICIDH defines 'impairment' as a biological condition, 'disability' as the functional limitations resulting from impairment, and 'handicap' as the social consequences of impairment and disability (WHO, 1980). It can be said that how disability is defined and understood as a concept can have fundamental implications for the framing of policies or for the way disability prevalence is measured. Thus a theoretical definition of disability can have far reaching social, economic, and political implications (Mitra, 2006).

The CRPD describes persons with disabilities as 'someone who has long-term physical, mental, intellectual or sensory impairments which in interaction with various barriers may hinder their full and effective participation in society on an equal basis with others' (United Nations, 2006: p. 4). For the study presented in this chapter, we used the definition of disability provided in the CRPD as a guiding framework during the analysis of the interviews. This is because the CRPD definition reflects the social model of disability, which emphasises the need for social change to remove disabling barriers while acknowledging the relevance of medical treatment of impairments (Barnes & Mercer, 2004). Considering that the CRPD a key milestone for inclusive education internationally, we used the CRPD's definition as a benchmark in order to understand how our participants' understanding of disability might relate (or not) to the definition outlined in the CRPD. We were also wondering to what extent Bhutanese people's understanding of disability would reflect western discourses and to what extent other local discourses would emerge from their responses.

3.3.2   'Inclusion'

Inclusion in education or inclusive education has been at the core of educational discourse for the last three decades and it has now established firm roots in the education system of many countries around the world (Hodkinson, 2010). The early move towards inclusion started in the mid-1980s and early 1990s and originated from different groups of people, such as for example parents, teachers and advocates, who were critical of existing educational provision for children with disabilities and advocated a shift towards inclusion as a strategy to challenge the barriers experienced by those children in education in terms of access and participation (Armstrong, Armstrong, & Spandagou, 2010). The placement of disabled learners in segregated education settings has also been found to be detrimental to their social and economic inclusion by perpetuating their isolation and reinforcing longstanding negative stereotypes (Metts, 2004). More recently, policy documents and international declarations such as the Salamanca Statement (UNESCO, 1994), CRPD, and the United Nations' Sustainable Development Goals have driven the policy and practice of inclusive education around the world.

It is accepted that inclusion is a complex concept that could mean different things to different people. It is therefore not surprising that a great deal of disagreement and confusion exists on how inclusion in education should be defined (Farrell & Ainscow, 2002). Booth (1999) defines inclusion in education as a process of reducing the exclusion of learners from curricula, cultures and communities by increasing their participation. Ainscow (2005) described inclusion as a never-ending process of finding better ways of responding to diversity and focusing on the identification and removal of barriers. He moreover states that inclusion is about the presence, participation and achievement of all. Norwich (2005) considers inclusion as more of an orienting term on a set of issues and commitments around belonging and participation. From Norwich's perspective, even special schools could be as inclusive as mainstream schools or ideally could be more inclusive than mainstream schools. It all boils down to the ethos of the school and the everyday classroom practices employed by the teachers.

In general terms, inclusion is seen by many as a philosophy of acceptance where all people are valued and treated with respect and where they feel and behave as full members of the community (Booth, 1999; Bouck, 2006; Carrington & Robinson, 2004; Topping & Maloney, 2005). In practice this means that all pupils, irrespective of their individual differences should be able to access the mainstream curriculum successfully, but may need support, individual adaptations or some kind of differentiation. According to Norwich (2008), inclusion is about restructuring mainstream schools to fit the needs of all children and it encourages the whole school to become more adaptable and inclusive in its day-to-day educational practices.

Given the very specific contextual characteristics of Bhutan, like the principle of GNH, that is based on Buddhist values described previously, we were wondering how the above broad definitions of inclusion are reflected or not on how Bhutanese people understand inclusion; and how Bhutanese people conceptualise inclusion more broadly.

3.4   Inclusion and Disability in Bhutan

Bhutan is primarily an agrarian country where 70–80% of the population lives in the villages. In the past, many disabled people played their role in their daily lives by working in the field, looking after cattle or doing domestic chores. Because the agrarian lifestyle demands physical labour, in this context one's ability to build, cultivate and do physical task was considered important and valued much more than an individual's ability to memorise, read, write and synthesise knowledge. Hence the concept of ability or disability in Bhutan was originally determined by one's ability to do physical work or domestic tasks and not by the ability to read and write. As a result, those with mild learning or physical disabilities were included members of the community, but those with severe intellectual and developmental disabilities, who were not able to take part in labour or everyday household chores were marginalised and often experienced social exclusion (Schuelka, 2013).

Hence prior to the modernisation era and the introduction of western education principles and structures, literacy and mental skills were not considered important and had little impact on the everyday life of Bhutan's citizens. Dorji (2015) argues that the concept of disability in Bhutan was and still is, to some extent, largely shaped by the functional capabilities of one's body and the ability to perform socially defined roles. Special Education only began in Bhutan with the work of Prince Namgyel Wangchuck (the younger brother of the late third King), when he served as a patron to the country's first special school in Khaling, in Trashigang district, in 1973. While the school was segregated from the mainstream schools, it has played a significant role in changing the attitudes of the general population, and influencing the commitment to the development of inclusive education that is seen today in Bhutan. In 2000, the Royal Government of Bhutan undertook a very significant initiative to make education more accessible to children with disabilities by establishing a Special Education Unit under the Education Department, which was upgraded as a separate division in 2011 (MoE, 2012). Following the establishment of SEN Unit in 2000, the Ministry of Education in 2002 identified a school in Thimphu (the capital city of Bhutan) as being ready to accept children with mild disabilities (MoE, 2013) and proposed to increase the number of schools with SEN programmes to 15 by the end of 11th Five Year Plan, 2018 (MoE, 2012). Moreover Article 9.15 of the Constitution of Bhutan advocates for inclusion as follows:

> The State shall endeavour to provide education for the purpose of improving and increasing knowledge, values and skills of the entire population with education being directed towards the full development of the human personality. (2008: 19–20)

Another noteworthy step that Bhutan in general and the Royal University of Bhutan in particular took in the move towards inclusion was the introduction of a module on "Teaching children with special needs" for a Bachelor's degree for Primary Education students at the two colleges of education (Paro College of Education and Samtse College of Education). The Paro College of Education, in partnership with the country's UNICEF office, is also currently working on developing a postgraduate level programme on Inclusive Education aimed at furthering the training of school leaders and teachers, and the first author of this chapter is involved in this work (Paro College of Education, 2013). In the meantime, efforts are also been made to make school infrastructures more accessible for children with disabilities. For instance, ramps for independent mobility of children with visual and physical disabilities are constructed in selected schools and public places. However, when it comes to the education of children with disabilities, the Bhutan government still adopts a 'continuum-oriented system', where both the special education and inclusive education systems exist alongside each other much like in Western contexts like for example England that maintain segregated school settings despite their rhetorical commitment to inclusion (Norwich, 2008).

While it is important to applaud the progress that Bhutan has made in terms of making inclusive education part of its education policy, the outcomes of its practice in the field have been less tangible. For instance, the 2015 Annual Education Statistics report shows that 1.2% of children are still out of school. The worrying part is that among those who are out of school, the majority of them are expected to be children with mild or those with hidden disabilities. Other research findings also show children with disabilities as being at the highest risk of marginalisation and being out of school (e.g. Graham, 2014; WHO, 2011). There are also many other challenges that Bhutan is facing in terms of inclusion in education of children with disabilities that are worthy of mention.

Considering that Bhutan is largely a Buddhist country (Maxwell, 2008), it can be expected that many Bhutanese people would attribute disability to the concept of karma, a belief that people are reincarnated or reborn into different forms of life depending upon their deeds from past lives (for an extensive discussion of this, see Kamenopoulou & Dukpa, 2017). Giffard-Lindsay (2007) highlighted that in developing countries, disability is often seen as a product of past karma and those born with disabilities as the subject of charity or welfare. For example, the Indian society seems to hold the view that by giving charity to people with disabilities believed to be born disabled, because of their past life sins, they can improve their own karma for the next life. A study carried out by UNICEF Bhutan (2012) found out that many parents of children with disabilities in Bhutan attribute having children with disabilities to their bad fate (or past life karma). This belief in karma seems to have a huge bearing on how people with disabilities are treated in Bhutan, in that they are frequently considered to have been responsible for their own fate (Schuelka, 2012).

Hence it must be acknowledged that the association of faith and karma with the causes of a disability can be problematic in the conceptualisation of disability (Schuelka, 2012). However, as Miles (2000) points out, the belief in karma does not have to be perceived as negative or contradictory to inclusion, because:

> For the western audience, the notion of karma may more usefully be packaged not as inescapable doom or retributive fate, but as a neutral, chastening, educational force. (611)

Another issue that is prevalent in Bhutan is the medicalisation of disability by the wider population. Giffard-Lindsay (2007) reported a similar scenario in India where the medical model of disability seems to be the cultural norm. This conceptualisation of disability as a medical condition is a major issue especially in developing countries such as Bhutan, because it can significantly influence, and perhaps determine the type of services designed for people with disabilities or the approach for supporting them in different contexts like education, work, etc. Disability is likely to be still widely regarded by the wider Bhutanese population as a problem to be cured so that a person with disability can be made 'more normal'. This can be a major obstacle in the move towards inclusion, because as mentioned before, locating the problem within an individual does now allow for the conceptualisation of disability also in relation to the barriers posed by the environment.

Another major challenge Bhutan is facing in terms of including children with disabilities in mainstream schools is the ranking of schools based on academic performance of the students. Again this scenario is similar to that reported in schools in the United Kingdom (Farrell & Ainscow, 2002), which are faced with the challenge of including children with special needs on the one hand and raising academic standards on the other. Schools are judged and placed into league tables on the basis of academic performance (Warnock, 2010) and this is also the case in Bhutan where the success and image of the schools are judged by the academic performance of the students. In practice, this means that the least academically strong children, a lot of whom tend to have disabilities and/or special needs, influence their schools' performance in a negative way. This is a major issue, because school ranking based on the test based academic performance of students can work against the inclusion of children with disabilities (Pinnock & Kaplan, 2014).

Finally, we were motivated to carry out this research due to the lack of local research in the field of disability and inclusion (Gyamtsho & Maxwell, 2012). According to Wangmo (2013), the dearth of research in the field of teacher education and inclusion, in the context of Bhutan makes it imperative for professionals to spearhead research that is contextually relevant to Bhutan. Sharma, Forlin, Deppeler, and Guang-xue (2013) cite lack of published research in the field of inclusion in developing countries as the main challenge in understanding the situation of inclusive education in those countries. Graham (2014) also cites lack of separate data on children with disabilities as one of the biggest obstacles to understanding the barriers that these children face in many developing countries.

Considering that the literature points to having contextually applicable empirical knowledge as being vital in ensuring the inclusion of persons with disabilities in education, the study that we conducted aimed to explore and capture the concepts 'Disability' and 'Inclusion' as seen through the perspective of Bhutanese people. We wanted to answer the following questions: How do Bhutanese people conceptualise disability? How do they understand inclusion? The following section outlines the methodology we used for our study.

3.5   METHODOLOGY

Part of the data used for this research had been collected for the first author's EMSIE Dissertation project that focused on the perspectives of Bhutanese teachers. After the dissertation was completed, we decided to expand the research and conducted a series of additional interviews with both teachers and other locals, because we wanted to reach more diverse groups. Hence the study we present in this chapter is an extension of the one already carried out as part of the first author's dissertation project.

The rationale was to construct an understanding of inclusion and disability from a Bhutanese perspective and give a range of locals the opportunity to share their understanding of these concepts. We used the semi-structured interview method to collect our data. Fourteen questions invited participants to give their understanding of inclusion, disability, challenges to inclusion, qualities of an inclusive educator and understanding of the links between inclusion and disability. The overarching aim as stated before was to construct the concepts 'disability' and 'inclusion' that are contextually relevant to people in Bhutan.

A list of participants' characteristics (i.e. age and gender) is provided in Table 3.1. Before the interview was conducted, participants were informed that their participation in the study was voluntary and that they had the right to withdraw at any stage, after which they each signed an informed consent form. To maintain the anonymity and confidentiality of the participants, instead of their real names, we used code names and in this chapter we only describe participants according to their background where relevant (Table 3.2).

Table 3.1 Participants' characteristics

Gender	Number
Male	8
Female	7
Total	15
Age range	**Number**
Under 25	3
25–35	7
35–45	2
45–55	2
55–65	1
Total	15

Table 3.2 Participants' background

Occupation/background	Number
Teacher in a school with SEN programme	3
Teacher in a general school	3
Teacher educator at a college	1
Trainee teacher	2
Parent of a child with disability	2
Medical doctor	1
Civil engineer	1
Monk in Buddhist college	1
Parliamentarian	1
Total	15

3.6   PRESENTATION OF FINDINGS

Guided by the research questions, data was analysed by identifying the key ideas or themes from the interview transcripts (Braun & Clarke, 2008). Accordingly, the results were grouped under 3 main themes:

1. Perception of inclusion
2. Perception of disability
3. Perception of the relationship between disability and inclusion.

The findings are presented in the following section under each of these themes.

3.6.1   *Perception of Inclusion*

In answer to our question 'What is your understanding of the concept 'inclusion in education or inclusive education'?' It is significant we feel that almost everyone (14 out of 15 participants) mentioned people with disabilities when they were giving their definition or understanding of inclusion. Below are some illustrative definitions we gathered:

> Inclusion is a concept where these people [people with disabilities] are actively encouraged and included as equal citizens. (Doctor)

> Inclusion secures opportunities for students with disabilities to learn alongside their non-disabled peers. (Trainee teacher)

> To include person[s] with disabilities. (Grade VI student)

> I think inclusion is to include persons with disabilities in the society by giving them special education. (monk in Buddhist college)

Furthermore, their understandings of inclusion seemed to be influenced by their professional background. For instance teacher participants understood inclusion as the mainstream placement of children with disabilities, as captured by the following definition:

> Inclusion is taking care of children with disabilities and educating them along with other children who are not disabled. (Lecturer who is also a parent of a child with disability)

Few participants also gave definitions of inclusion as a human right and also expressed the view that no one should be deprived of that right. For example:

Every child is entitled to inclusive education. (Teacher in school with SEN programme)

Inclusion is making sure that they [people with disabilities] have equal fundamental rights as any other citizen (Doctor)

A broader view of inclusion as concerning all people was only described by one participant, who is a Member of Parliament in Bhutan:

Including everyone in the group or mainstream irrespective of certain conditions that individuals suffer from- without discrimination.

3.6.2   Perception of Disability

When we asked participants 'what is your understanding of the term 'disability' and 'can you give description of a person whom you would consider as 'disabled'?' participants strongly associated disability with a medical condition and also described being disabled as being different from the norm. Moreover, some participants seemed to strongly associate disability with lack of ability and deficit. In Table 3.3 we summarised some of the descriptions given by participants of 'disability' and of 'a disabled' person.

In order to delve deeper into the participants' understanding of disability, we asked them what in their view are the main causes of disability and what they think makes a person disabled. Most of the participants (except the one who was a medical doctor) mentioned medications, accidents, genetics, carelessness of the parents, unhealthy lifestyle, illness etc. as main causes of disability (see Table 3.4).

Like we had anticipated, some participants also associated disability with fate and past karma. For example:

I think disability is caused mainly because someone did not accumulate enough merit in their past life...also may be in the past life the person must have thought evil, intended harm and been unkind to others.

Table 3.3 Participants' definition of 'disability'/'disabled person'

Definitions given
'…disabled children are not able to do things like other people or other children'. (P1)
'[Disabled is] someone who cannot walk properly, someone who cannot speak properly, someone who cannot hear properly' (P2)
'[Disability is] a condition where a person is physically, mentally or intellectually challenged…'
'[Disabled] is someone who is visually impaired, speech, impaired, autistic, challenged with physical movement, mentally impaired' (P15)
'[Disabled is] a person who is not capable of performing basic necessity tasks on a day to day basis'. (P8)
'From my understanding, the term 'disability' means someone who lacks the adequate strength physical and mental capability'. (P6)
'Disabled is the person who cannot walk and is on the wheel chair, who is semi or totally blind, who cannot talk and is dumb, who can't hear and is deaf.' (P9)
'[Disabled is] someone who is blind, deaf or without arms and legs. (P12)

Table 3.4 Participants' beliefs about what causes disability

'The main cause of disability in terms of physical disability could be biological and medical'….. 'diet and genes, ….accident.' (P3)
'Firstly when the mother is careless and she abuses unhealthy things when the child is in the womb and after birth when the child is not provided with proper diet.' (P7)
'Disability is mainly caused by illness like heart disease, injuries, obesity.' (P10)
'When a pregnant mother does not take care of fetus.' (P11)
'Carelessness of the parents of the newborn, unhealthy lifestyle, accidents etc.' (P14)
'Teenage pregnancy and complications during pregnancy-drinking alcohol, smoking and taking medicines against doctor's advice.' (P15)

Not surprisingly, this statement comes from the participant who is a Buddhist monk. However, there were others who held similar views:

> I think some people are born disabled probably because of the past karma or fate.

The only participant who looked at disability from a social model perspective was a medical doctor. He also talked about how impairment and disability are two different concepts. Here is what he said:

> The main cause [of disability] is how society views these people, who are differently abled. That is the problem, the cause of the impairment would be

apparent like trauma, childhood conditions, genetic, etc., but what makes a person "disabled" is how the society portrays them and treats them as a second grade people who are incapable of anything. It is the issue of misguided views.

3.6.3   Perception of the Relationship Between 'Inclusion' and 'Disability'

In response our question 'From your perspective, what is the relationship between 'disability' and 'inclusion'?' almost everyone viewed them as related concepts as it is evident from the following quotations:

[Inclusion is about] including an individual with disabilities in everyday activities and encouraging them to have roles similar to the ones who do not have any disability. (P14)

When we consider the inclusion, there we consider the disabled person. (P7)

Disability is the consequence of the impairment as society perceives it and inclusion is the movement to include these people into society to treat them with equality, justice and non-discriminately. (P9)

It is important to note that in answer to this question some participants shared their concerns regarding the viability of inclusion of disabled children in the context of Bhutan, and here is an illustrative quotation:

In my opinion, in our country inclusive education is not very appropriate because teachers [who are teaching in mainstream schools] are not qualified or trained in special education and also there is lack of infrastructure and teaching learning material and more over those with disabilities are not able to keep up with those without disabilities which may affect their self-esteem and confidence and lead to frustrations. (P15)

3.7   Summary of Findings

Our findings strongly suggest that participants tended to construct disability from a medical model perspective, according to which they perceived it as a product of genetic inheritance, medical condition, accidents and other reasons related to an individual's health and wellbeing. They also saw disability as being different from the norm and as needing treatment and medication. Not surprisingly, some participants also associated disability with fate and past karma. In terms of inclusion, participants understood the concept as meaning mainstreaming or including children with disability in school alongside other children who are not identified as having disability. Some participants also shared their view that inclusion may not be the best choice for a developing country like Bhutan citing reasons such as lack of resources, lack of trained teachers and lack of wider disability awareness.

3.8   Conclusions and Recommendations

The findings from our study suggest that overall the Bhutanese people interviewed understood disability from a perspective that differs from the one proposed in the CRPD and is closer to the medical model perspective in that they perceived disability as being the product of factors that lie within the disabled person. Overwhelmingly, participants viewed disability as something that needs to be cured, rehabilitated, and fixed (Barnes & Mercer, 2004). Kroeger (2010) reminds us that in Western societies prior to the era of the disability movement in the 70s and the social model of disability (which viewed disability as the consequence of factors that are external to the individual like societal barriers), disability was seen as arising from the physical, sensory, emotional or cognitive limitations of an individual. Findings from our study interestingly reveal a conceptualisation of disability that is similar to the view of disability as caused by the limitations of an individual, i.e. by within person factors. Moreover, we noted in the narratives that we collected that participants saw people with disabilities through a quite patronising lens, describing them as less abled, less normal and in need of care by the more abled people. They also held the view that the parents of disabled children were responsible for their children's disability and indeed the causes of disability were frequently associated with a pregnant mother's bad habits. Schuelka (2014, 2015) following his ethnographic study on the perception of disability in Bhutan reported very similar findings.

Conceptualising disability from a medical model perspective can be detrimental when designing policies, services and provisions for people with disabilities. For example, seeing disability as located within an individual who needs to be cured will result in resources and policies being directed towards providing medical treatment or normalising the individual rather than working on changing the environment and providing services and support. Moreover, as explained earlier in the chapter, this medical view of disability contradicts both the principle of GNH and the inclusive philosophy.

Some of the participants also understood disability as being a product of past karma or fate. Relevant literature points out that in developing countries disability is often seen as a product of previous sins and those born with disabilities as subject of charity (see Giffard-Lindsay, 2007). Attributing the cause of disability to fate or karma can be problematic when pursuing inclusion, because a society that conceptualises disability as a product of fate generally believes that disability of an individual is determined by their destiny and that there is little that society can do to support that individual. Schuelka (2014, 2015) argues that the notion of past life actions determining the present life circumstances could lead to a general mistrust and blame placed on the person with a disability. However, he also notes that Bhutanese GNH-influenced policies based on Buddhist philosophies cultivate compassion and are supportive of persons with disabilities and in line with the wider principles behind inclusion, and this is also supported by Miles (1995, 2000).

It is worth mentioning that one participant understood disability from a social model perspective and mentioned that impairment and disability are two different concepts. He stated that the main cause of disability is how the society treats people with disability and that an individual's impairment doesn't necessarily result in disablement. His view of disability seemed to be more aligned with the definition adopted by the CRPD. As mentioned earlier, the CRPD describes persons with disabilities as people with 'long-term physical, mental, intellectual or sensory impairments, which in interaction with various barriers may hinder their full and effective participation in society on an equal basis with others' (United Nations, 2006: p. 4). Schuelka (2014, 2015) found that the rights model or the social model is influential in the construction of disability in Bhutan at the same time as the medical model; and in another study, we also came up with very similar conclusions (Kamenopoulou & Dukpa, 2017). Given that the only participant in our study who held a social model view was a highly educated person and member of the parliament, we feel compelled to highlight the possible role of education, social class and professional background in the way people in Bhutan conceptualise disability and inclusion.

Another interesting finding was that almost all participants associated the notion of inclusion or inclusive education with pupils with disabilities.

Participants mostly described inclusion as meaning mainstreaming or including children with disability in school alongside other children who are not identified as having disability. This understanding of inclusion can be seen as problematic for two reasons. Firstly, because literature has long established that inclusive education is not only about the physical placement of children with disabilities in mainstream schools but providing the right support that will enable their full participation in the school life (see for example Ainscow, 2005). Moreover, a view that has been getting increasing acceptance in recent years is that inclusion does not only concern those children with disabilities, but many other vulnerable groups of children, who are at risk for exclusion from education. Inclusion is about presence, participation and accommodation of all students (Ainscow, 2005). Within this framework, participants' understanding of inclusion can be described as somewhat narrow or superficial, and again does not reflect the broader definitions that we highlighted earlier in the chapter (see Ainscow, 2005; Giffard-Lindsay, 2007; Norwich, 2005). The idea of inclusive education as focused on the physical placement of children with disabilities was first introduced by the Salamanca statement (UNESCO, 1994). Hence from an early stage, the notion of inclusion has been associated with those children with disabilities. Different sources suggest that the view of inclusion as associated with the physical placement of these specific children still survives today in many contexts, including the global North and South (see Hodkinson, 2010; Kamenopoulou & Dukpa, 2017; Sikes, Lawson, & Parker, 2007; Zoniou-Sideri & Vlachou, 2006). Our findings seem to support this, and it seems that in Bhutan people tend to see mere placement of children with disabilities in a mainstream school as a synonym for inclusion.

It is also worth mentioning that some participants shared that inclusion may not be the best choice for a developing country like Bhutan citing reasons such as lack of resources, lack of teacher training on inclusive education and lack of disability awareness. Similarly Le Fanu (2013) argued that many education systems in developing countries face inadequate resources, low quality teacher training and large class sizes and consequently questioned whether it is possible to achieve inclusion within these contexts. Schuelka (2014) also found teacher under-preparedness to address diverse learning needs of students as major obstacle in the move towards inclusion in Bhutan, and in our study on Bhutanese teachers' perspectives, we had similar findings (Kamenopoulou & Dukpa, 2017). According to a breadth of literature, successful implementation of inclusion depends to a large extend on the attitude and level of teacher competence. The key role teachers' play in implementing inclusive practices implies that how teachers conceptualise and understand the concepts 'inclusion' and 'disability' will have significant implications on the successful implementation of inclusive approaches (Mitra, 2006). Since teachers are the ones who are implementing inclusive practices in the schools, they are the key change agents in any inclusive development (e.g. Carrrington & Robinson, 2004; Dorji & Schuelka, 2016; Kamenopoulou, Buli-Holmberg, & Siska, 2015). Schuelka (2013) usefully observed that when it comes to teaching a diverse range of learners, most Bhutanese teachers are under-trained, under resourced and under supported. More recently, Dorji and Schuelka (2016) also stressed the lack of trained teachers to implement inclusion in Bhutan.

We therefore argue that our findings call for better translation of policies into practices, i.e. improved training programmes for teachers in Bhutan and disability awareness programmes for the wider population. Unfortunately however, our findings also seem to suggest that the journey towards inclusion in Bhutan is still at its infancy stage. It seems that people in Bhutan are only just beginning to grasp the ideas and theoretical concepts behind inclusive education, and a part of the population is not aware of the benefits of inclusion and understand it in many different ways. Overall, we hope that our findings will be used to better educate Bhutanese people about inclusion and disability. Finally, findings from our study also support the view that concepts like *inclusion* and *disability* can be understood and interpreted in many different ways in different contexts (Farrell & Ainscow, 2002). This is particularly true in the context of Bhutan, where cultural beliefs about karma seem to influence how Bhutanese people think about disability and inclusion. Understanding the abstract nature of these concepts and how they may be seen differently in different contexts should help policy makers to frame appropriate policies and practitioners to engage in practices that take into consideration these local factors (Kamenopoulou & Dukpa, 2017).

Lack of systematic research in the context of Bhutan has been one of the biggest challenges for academics and professionals, who wish to engage in further enquiry and self-development in the areas of inclusion and disability. The findings from our study will help expand the limited knowledge that is contextually relevant to Bhutan.

REFERENCES

Ainscow, M. (2005). Understanding the development of inclusive education system. *Electronic Journal of Research in Educational Psychology, 3*(3), 5–20.

Armstrong, A. C., Armstrong, D., & Spandagou, I. (2010). *Inclusive education, international policy and practice*. London: Sage Publications Ltd.

Barnes, C. (2000). A working social model? Disability, work and disability politics in the 21st century. *Critical Social Policy, 20*(4), 441–456.

Barnes, C., & Mercer, G. (2004). Theorising and researching disability from a social model perspective. In C. Barnes & G. Mercer (Eds.), *Implementing the social model of disability: Theory and research* (pp. 1–17). Leeds: The Disability Press.

Barnes, C., & Mercer, G. (2005). Understanding impairment and disability: Towards an international perspective. In C. Barnes & G. Mercer (Eds.), *The social model of disability and the majority world* (pp. 1–16). Leeds: The Disability Press.

Booth, T. (1999). Viewing inclusion from a distance: Gaining perspective from comparative study. *Support for Learning, 14*(4), 164–168.

Bouck, E. C. (2006). Spotlight on inclusion: What research and practice is telling the field. *Electronic Journal for Inclusive Education, 1*(10), 1–22.

Braun, V., & Clarke, V. (2008). Using thematic analysis in psychology. *Qualitative Research in Psychology, 3*(2), 77–101.

Carrington, S., & Robinson, R. (2004). A case study of inclusive school development: A journey of learning. *The International Journal of Inclusive Education, 8*(2), 141–153.

Dorji, R. (2015). Teaching social skills to children with Autism Spectrum Disorder (ASD): A case study of selected mainstream primary schools in the Borough of London, UK. *RABSEL the Centre for Educational Research and Development Journal, 16*(2), 18–36.

Dorji, R., & Schuelka, M. J. (2016). Children with disabilities in Bhutan: Transitioning from special educational needs to inclusive education. In M. J. Schuelka & T. W. Maxwell (Eds.), *Education in Bhutan: Culture, schooling and gross national happiness* (pp. 181–198). Singapore: Springer Science.

Farrell, P., & Ainscow, M. (2002). Making special education inclusive: Mapping the issues. In P. Farrell & M. Ainscow (Eds.), *Making special education inclusive* (pp. 1–12). London: David Fulton.

Giffard-Lindsay, K. (2007). *Inclusive education in India: Interpretation, implementation, and issues*. Project Report. Consortium for Research on Educational Access, Transitions and Equity (CREATE). Falmer, UK.

Graham, N. (2014). Children with disabilities. Paper commissioned for *Fixing the broken promise of education for all: Findings from the global initiative on out-of-school children* (UIS/UNICEF, 2015), Montreal: UNESCO Institute for Statistics (UIS).

Gyamstho, D. C., & Maxwell, T. W. (2012). Present practices and background to teaching and learning at the Royal University of Bhutan (RUB): A pilot study. *International Journal of Teaching and Learning in Higher Education, 24*(1), 65–75.

Hodkinson, A. (2010). Inclusive and special education in the English educational system: Historical perspectives, recent developments and future challenges. *British Journal of Special Education, 37*(2), 61–67.

Kamenopoulou, L., Buli-Holmberg, J., & Siska, J. (2015). An exploration of student teachers' perspectives at the start of a post-graduate study programme on inclusion and special needs education. *International Journal of Inclusive Education, 20*(7), 743–755.

Kamenopoulou, L., & Dukpa, D. (2017). Karma and human rights: Bhutanese teachers' perspectives on inclusion and disability. *International Journal of Inclusive Education.* https://doi.org/10.1080/13603116.2017.1365274

Kroeger, S. (2010). From the special issue editor. *Journal of Postsecondary Education and Disability, 23*(1), 3–4.

Le Fanu, G. (2013). Reconceptualizing inclusive education in international development. In L. Tikly & A. M. Barrett (Eds.), *Education quality and social justice in the global South: Challenges for policy, practice and research.* London: Routledge.

Maxwell, T. W. (2008). The important issues facing children in the Kingdom of Bhutan. In I. Epstein & J. Pattnaik (Eds.), *The Greenwood encyclopaedia of children's issues worldwide: Asia and Oceania* (pp. 55–77). New York: Greenwood Press.

Metts, R. (2004). *Disability and development background paper for the disability and development research agenda meeting.* Washington, DC: World Bank Headquarters. Retrieved from http://siteresources.worldbank.org/DISABILITY/Resources/280658-1172606907476/mettsBGpaper.pdf

Metts, R. L. (2000). Disability issues, trends and recommendations for the World Bank. Online. Retrieved from http://siteresources.worldbank.org/DISABILITY/Resources/280658-1172606907476/DisabilityIssuesMetts.pdf

Miles, M. (1995). Disability in an Eastern religious context: Historical perspectives. *Disability & Society, 10*(1), 49–70.

Miles, M. (2000). Disability on a different model: Glimpses of an Asian heritage. *Disability & Society, 15*(4), 603–618.

Ministry of Education. (2012). *National policy on special educational needs* (final draft). Royal Government of Bhutan.

Ministry of Education. (2013). *Annual education statistics.* Thimphu, Bhutan: Policy and Planning Division, Ministry of Education, Royal Government of Bhutan.

Ministry of Education. (2014). *Bhutan education blueprint 2014–2024.* Thimphu, Bhutan: Ministry of Education, Royal Government of Bhutan.

Ministry of Education. (2015). *Annual education statistics.* Thimphu, Bhutan: Policy and Planning Division, Ministry of Education, Royal Government of Bhutan.

Ministry of Education. (2017). *Standards for inclusive education.* Thimphu, Bhutan: Ministry of Education, Royal Government of Bhutan.

Mitra, S. (2006). The capability approach and disability. *Journal of Disability Policy Studies, 16*(4), 236–247.

National Statistics Bureau. (2013). *Statistical year book of Bhutan.* Thimphu: National Statistics Bureau, Royal Government of Bhutan.

Norwich, B. (2005). Inclusion: Is it a matter of evidence about what works or about values and rights? *International Journal of Primary, Elementary and Early Years Education, 33*(1), 51–56.

Norwich, B. (2008). *Dilemmas of difference, inclusion and disability.* London: Routledge.

Paro College of Education. (2013). *Strategic plan (2013–2020).* Royal University of Bhutan.

Phuntsho, K. (2000). Two ways of learning. *Journal of Bhutan Studies, 2*(2), 96–126.

Pinnock, H., & Kaplan, I. (2014). *Meeting the educational needs of children with disabilities in South Asia: A gap analysis covering Bhutan and the Maldives.* United Nations Chidren's Fund, Regional Office for South Asia. Retrieved May 01, 2017, from http://www.eenet.org.uk/resources/docs/UNICEF%20 ROSA_Disabilities_Gap_Analysis_BhutanMaldives.pdf

Ralston, C., & Hoe, J. (2010). Philosophical reflection on disability. In C. Ralston & J. Hoe (Eds.), *Philosophical reflection on disability.* New York: Springer Science + Business Media.

Royal Government of Bhutan. (2008). *The constitution of the Kingdom of Bhutan.* Retrieved May 1, 2017, from http://www.constitution

Schuelka, M. J. (2012). Inclusive education in Bhutan: A small state with alternative priorities. *Current Issues in Comparative Education, 15*(1), 145–156.

Schuelka, M. J. (2013). Education for youth with disabilities in Bhutan: Past, present, and future. *Bhutan Journal of Research and Development, 2*(1), 65–74.

Schuelka, M. J. (2014). Constructing disability in Bhutan: Schools, structures, policies and global discourses. A dissertation submitted to the faculty of the Graduate School, University of Minnesota, USA.

Schuelka, M. J. (2015). The evolving construction and conceptualisation of 'disability' in Bhutan. *Disability & Society, 30*(6), 820–833.

Sharma, U., Forlin, C., Deppeler, J., & Guang-xue. (2013). Reforming teacher education for inclusion in developing countries in the Asia-Pacific region. *Asian Journal of Inclusive Education, 1*(1), 3–16.

Sikes, P., Lawson, H., & Parker, M. (2007). Voices on: Teachers and teaching assistants talk about inclusion. *International Journal of Inclusive Education, 11*(3), 355–370.

Topping, K., & Maloney, S. (2005). Introduction. In K. Topping & S. Maloney (Eds.), *The Routledge Falmer reader in inclusive education* (pp. 1–12). London: Routledge Falmer; Taylor & Francis Group.

UNESCO. (1994). *Salamanca statement and framework for action*. Paris: UNESCO.

UNICEF. (2012). *Rights, Education and Protection (REAP), third progress report*. Bhutan: UNICEF.

United Nations. (1993). *Standard rules on the equalization of opportunities for people with disabilities*. New York: UN.

United Nations. (2006). *Convention on the rights of persons with disabilities*. New York: UN.

Ura, K., & Galay, K. (Eds.). (2004). *Gross national happiness and development: Proceedings of the first international seminar on operationalising gross national happiness*. Thimphu, Bhutan: Centre for Bhutan Studies.

Wangmo, P. (2013). *An investigation of phonological processing and reading skills in Bhutanese primary students*. PhD thesis, University of Newcastle, Australia.

Warnock, M. (2010). Special education needs: A new look. In L. Terzi (Ed.), *Special educational needs: A new look*. London: Continuum International Publishing Group.

World Health Organisation. (1980). *International classification of impairments, disabilities and handicaps*. Geneva: WHO.

World Health Organization. (2011). *World report on disability*. Geneva: WHO. Retrieved from www.who.int/disabilities/world_report/2011/report/en/

Zoniou-Sideri, A., & Vlachou, A. (2006). Greek teachers' belief systems about disability and inclusive education. *International Journal of Inclusive Education, 10*(4), 379–394.

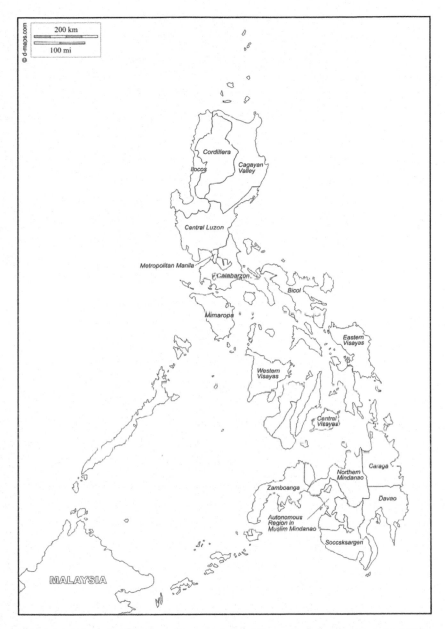

Fig. 4.1 Map of Philippines (Source: http://www.d-maps.com/m/asia/philippines/philippines14.gif)

Teachers' Assessment Strategies for Children with Disabilities: A Constructivist Study in Mainstream Primary Schools in Negros Oriental, Philippines

Rolando Jr. C. Villamero and Leda Kamenopoulou

Abstract Chapter 4 presents a research that gathered the voices of mainstream classroom teachers in Negros Oriental, Philippines regarding the strategies they use for the assessment of pupils with disabilities. There is limited systematic research on assessment strategies used for pupils with disabilities in the Philippines. A constructivist methodology was adopted, including semi-structured interviews with 3 teachers and classroom observations. Findings revealed that teachers used a variety of strategies, such as tests, observations, portfolios, and groupings. Furthermore, in delivering these strategies, teachers made further adaptations based on individual children's needs. The authors stress that when differentiating assessment, teachers need to consider numerous complex factors, and they highlight

R. Jr. C. Villamero (✉)
Unicef Kenya Country Office (KCO), Nairobi, Kenya

L. Kamenopoulou
University of Roehampton, London, UK

© The Author(s) 2018
L. Kamenopoulou (ed.), *Inclusive Education and Disability in the Global South*, https://doi.org/10.1007/978-3-319-72829-2_4

some characteristics of the Philippines context that hinder the adoption of inclusive approaches to assessment of pupils with disabilities.

Keywords Assessment • Differentiation • Pupils with disabilities • Teacher voices • Philippines

> *'Because of the limitations that a child with a disability may have either intellectually or physically, there is a big need to modify the whole assessment process for him. This is the only way of ensuring that everything I do for him is responsive and relevant to his needs as a child with a disability'.*
> *(Teacher participant)*

4.1   Introduction

There is very limited systematic research on assessment strategies used for pupils with disabilities in the context of the Philippines. The aim of the research presented in this chapter was to give a voice to teachers from the Negros Oriental province regarding the strategies they use for the assessment of pupils with disabilities. In discussing our findings, we highlight the particular characteristics of the Philippines education system that hinder or enable the adoption of more inclusive approaches to assessment of pupils' learning outcomes.

Both in theory and in practice, assessment is recognised as an important aspect of the teaching-learning process. This is manifested in education policies worldwide that emphasise the assessment process and set principles as to how it should be implemented in the classroom setting. The Philippines has been proactive in supporting appropriate assessment strategies for all learners: in 2012, the K to 12 Basic Education Programme was passed into law, which exemplifies the principles of inclusive education, growth and development, teaching and learning, and assessment (SEAMEO & INNOTECH, 2012).

However, in spite of major policy initiatives like this one, the Philippine education system faces major challenges especially in relation to the assessment of children with disabilities. A rigid curriculum that leads to rigid assessment strategies, classroom shortages, and unfavourable learning environments in general are three of the many causes of students dropping out from school (UNESCO, 2015). These factors are also very likely to cause children with disabilities to struggle in the mainstream education classes. It is important to emphasise however that in the context of global North countries such as the US, UK, and Australia, there is a breadth of research literature exemplifying the assessment practices of teachers in primary schools for children with disabilities. Baessa (2008) argues that there is a significant need for studies to focus on developing countries so that there is an equal balance of perspectives about issues pertinent to different contexts.

The study reported in this chapter explored how three mainstream primary school teachers in the Negros Oriental province assessed children with disabilities in their classrooms. In particular, it examined the different assessment strategies they used and how they used them in order to respond to the needs of children with disabilities. A constructivist methodology was adopted, which allowed us to understand the experiences of the participants, the meaning of those experiences being constructed by the participants themselves (Charmaz, 2006). Interviews with the teachers and a series of classroom observations were conducted as part of data collection for this research.

The findings revealed that a range of assessment tools were used by the teachers such as tests, observations, portfolios, and groupings. Furthermore, in delivering assessment tools to children with disabilities, the teachers modified the content and delivery based on the needs of each child. The content modification included the use of the child's native language, and the length and level of difficulty of the assessment. Moreover, the foci of delivery modification were proximity, peer support, use of technology, and duration. This suggests that in delivering the different types of assessment strategies, there is a variety of complex factors for teachers to consider in order to best respond to the needs of children with disabilities. These findings raise questions about the capacity of teachers to respond to the needs of children with disabilities, given the harsh reality of mainstream schools in the context of the Philippines, and in this chapter we will be addressing those questions.

We would like to emphasise from the outset that this study is a product of our commitment towards making inclusive education a reality especially in global South contexts. We know how challenging the implementation of inclusive education can be in some contexts, but it is important to note that there also exist ad hoc initiatives that ensure that children with disabilities are provided with a learning process that is responsive to their needs. However, how can these scattered examples of good practice be shared with the education community if they are not documented systematically and further explored? This was the main reason why we interviewed three teachers working with children with disabilities about their approaches to assessment. We are grateful to those teachers for agreeing to take part in our study and for making it happen.

4.2   ASSESSMENT OF CHILDREN WITH DISABILITIES IN THE PHILIPPINES: A BRIEF BACKGROUND

The Philippine education system fully recognises the importance of providing appropriate assessment to all learners. The Department of Education is committed to creating schools that are more inclusive and to overcoming the challenges associated with educating children with disabilities in mainstream schools. Specifically, an intensive training programme on inclusive education strategies for teachers has been organised with the aim of helping them effectively meet the needs children with disabilities (DepEd, 2015). This initiative seems to have positively influenced schools' practices on inclusive education specifically on the aspect of teachers' innovation and creativity when assessing children with disabilities in their classrooms. Moreover, as mentioned earlier, the K to 12 Basic Education Programme that was introduced in 2012 exemplifies the principles of inclusive education, growth and development, teaching and learning, and assessment (SEAMEO & INNOTECH, 2012). Specifically, in terms of assessment, the Programme recognises learner-centeredness and places emphasis on the role of the learning environment. Furthermore, the Programme's assessment process warrants the employment of a vast array of traditional and new assessment tools and techniques for a valid, reliable, and realistic assessment of learning (DepEd, 2012). Simply put, the K to 12 Basic Education Programme has been designed to address the diverse learner needs and may be adapted to fit specific learner groups also in relation to assessment approaches (SEAMEO & INNOTECH, 2012).

However, in spite of the fact that major policies like this one are in place, the Philippine education system is faced with major challenges that seem to be related to a number of factors. UNESCO (2015: p. 56) notes that rigid curriculum and assessment processes, classroom shortages, and unfavourable learning environment are three of the many causes of students dropping out from school. It adds that teachers especially in government schools are left with no other option but to 'teach to the test' and that written achievement tests determine the quality of performance of the schools and teachers. In a report published by GP Rehab, one of the teachers interviewed stated:

> I do not have much time and resources for differentiation. I have more than 40 children in class. I also have to cope with the number of chapters and lessons I have to cover and deliver before the national test comes. (2013: p. 45)

It follows that this situation causes children with disabilities to struggle in the mainstream class. As a result, some parents continue to express their disappointment about how their children are being taught and assessed. In the same report, a mother of a child with cerebral palsy shared the following experience:

> His teacher does not really care about his presence in class. He just goes to school and sits in class. The teacher does not provide other ways for him to answer his exams even if he cannot hold his pencil. He has to force himself to write. (GPRehab, 2013: p. 16)

The above challenges can also be translated into figures. As a whole, only two per cent of Philippine's children with disabilities are in school and the drop-out rate is high (DeptEd, 2012). In addition, according to GPRehab (2013: p. 10) in the Negros Oriental province two out of three children with disabilities enrolled in mainstream primary classes drop out after three months from the start of the school year. The remaining number has less than 30 per cent chance of progressing to the next level (GPRehab, 2013). In response to these challenges, certain organisations such as for example The Great Physician Rehabilitation Foundation (GPRehab) have been leading the advocacy on the rights of children with disabilities in Negros Oriental, by establishing inclusive education systems in identified primary schools in the province. This includes implementing activities such as parent and teacher training programmes, school-based disability awareness activities, and monitoring of the status and progress of children with disabilities. These initiatives have positively influenced schools' practices on inclusive education. Certain public primary schools from three municipalities in the province of Negros Oriental, for example, have been identified and recognised as 'inclusive schools' because of the teachers' efforts to establish inclusive education systems that accommodate all children and especially those with disabilities (GPRehab, 2013). In addition, these efforts have led to significant improvement of teachers' competence in teaching children with disabilities especially in the area of assessment. GPRehab (2013) asserts that certain teachers specifically in primary schools in Negros Oriental initiate modifications in assessment approaches within their classes. The following is an example of a 'success story':

> I have a child with cerebral palsy in my grade III class. Because of her spasticity, she has a hard time accomplishing writing activities in class. I have to make some modifications in my classroom instruction. For exams that require intensive writing, I only ask the child to do a verbal evaluation. For example in spelling, instead of making her write the words, she spells them verbally. (Ma, 2013: p. 6)

This highlights the need for innovation and creativity on the part of the teacher when assessing children with disabilities. Miles and Singal (2010) stress that it is empowering to see teachers from developing countries innovating for inclusive education so that they can effectively work with children with disabilities. They add that, indeed, teachers play an important role in making inclusive education a reality, and this is another reason that motivated us to capture the teachers' perspectives and voices in our study, which we describe in detail in the following section.

4.3   TEACHERS' ASSESSMENT STRATEGIES: A RESEARCH STUDY IN THE PHILIPPINES

The goal of our qualitative study was to explore how three selected teachers assessed children with disabilities in mainstream primary classrooms in Negros Oriental, Philippines. Specifically, our aim was to answer the following research question:

1. How do primary school teachers assess children with disabilities in the mainstream classroom?

For greater clarity, we broke down the main question into two sub-questions:

1.1. What assessment strategies do primary school teachers employ for children with disabilities in the mainstream classrooms?

1.2. How do primary school teachers deliver the assessment strategies for children with disabilities in the mainstream classrooms?

In order to substantially explore the answers to these questions, we adopted a constructivist methodology, which provided the framework for our study. This methodology was chosen firstly because it highlights the understanding of human experiences (Corbin & Strauss, 2008) and encourages the researcher to depend upon the views of the participants (Creswell, 2007). Secondly, this methodology 'assumes that the meaning of experiences and events are constructed by individuals, and therefore people construct the realities in which they participate' (Charmaz, 2006: p. 58), because 'reality is socially constructed' (Mertens, 2005: p. 12). Accordingly, we gathered the experiences of primary school teachers in relation to assessment strategies and how they employ these strategies for children with disabilities in their mainstream classroom.

1.3.1   Target Population and Sampling

This study focused on gathering the perspectives of teaches from rural areas in Negros Oriental, who have children with disabilities in their classrooms. The two main criteria for choosing the study participants were to have:

(a) children with identified disabilities enrolled in their classrooms and
(b) experience of practicing inclusive education and specifically assessment strategies for children with disabilities for at least three years.

We wanted to include a diversity of experiences and hence selected participants from different grade levels and schools. In total, three teachers were selected for the interviews, teaching in grade one, two and three respectively. It is important to clarify that the study was limited to primary school teachers because they have responsibility for the total educational programme and a duty of care for their group of students throughout the school day (SEAMEO & INNOTECH, 2012). It is also important to note that most of the training opportunities on inclusive education are given to primary school teachers in the Philippines, perhaps also in response to the fact that more and more children with disabilities are enrolled in primary schools (DepEd, 2012).

We sought the informed consent of the selected teachers with a brief activity, informing them of the details of the study, that their participation was voluntary and that they could refuse to take part or withdraw at a later stage. According to Marshall and Rossman (2011), we also considered participant *confidentiality and anonymity*, and accordingly any identifiable information such as names of schools and teachers has been removed from the final report. Finally, another important ethical consideration was the need for *reciprocity*, and we provided participants with 'thank you' tokens and as well as copies of the final report.

4.3.2   Research Tools

We used two constructivist data collection tools, namely, semi-structured interviews and observations (Charmaz, 2006), each of which served different yet equally important purposes especially in the triangulation of data (Creswell, 2007).

Semi-structured interviews were the primary method of data collection and an interview guide (or a list of topics/questions) was used (Patton, 2002). The interviews allowed us to gather 'in-depth and direct perspectives' (Kvale & Brinkmann, 2009: p. 38) from the teachers on how they assessed children with disabilities. The researcher's role during the interview was to facilitate the process and gather relevant information from the teachers using the interview questions as a starting point (Cohen, Manion, & Morrison, 2007). As a constructivist tool, semi-structured interviews should achieve in-depth exploration and this may require multiple interviews with the same participant. This was the reason why the interview process in this study was completed in two stages. In the first stage, the main interview was conducted after a series of 1–2 three-hour class observations. The aim of the interview was to discuss in-depth the topics/questions listed in the interview guide (see Table 4.1). The interviews were a structured process in a sense that the date and time of the sessions were scheduled ahead, and these were audio recorded to ensure clarity and accuracy of data. This usually lasted for more than 30 minutes. In the second stage, informal follow up interviews were conducted where necessary to clarify points that arose from the class observations. These were usually conducted over 5 to 10 minutes at break time.

Furthermore, we used direct observations as a second method of data collection, and more specifically, we conducted naturalistic observations of classroom sessions, in order to explore in a 'direct and natural manner' (Woods & Pratt, 2006: p. 102) how teachers employed assessment strategies

Table 4.1 Interview guide used

Questions

1. What instances require you, as a primary school teacher, to employ assessment strategies for a child with a disability in your classroom?
   i. *Are these instances more internal (intrinsic) or external (extrinsic)? Or a combination of both? What are these specific instances?*
   ii. *How do you deal with these instances?*
2. What are the different forms or characteristics of assessment strategies you, as a primary school teacher, employ for a child with a disability?
   i. *Do you give priorities in differentiating among the different assessment strategies? Or do you give equal importance to all of them? Why?*
   ii. *What forms or characteristics of assessment strategies do you employ for a child with a disability in your classroom?*
   iii. *Can you give specific examples of these specific assessment strategies you employ for a child with a disability in your classroom?*
3. How do you, as a teacher, deliver the assessment strategies for a child with a disability your classroom?
   i. *What aspects or criteria do you have to consider in delivering the assessment strategies for a child with a disability your classroom?*
   ii. *Do you have to utilize existing assessment materials and modify them? Or do you have to create new ones? Elaborate.*
   iii. *What specific strategies do you employ in delivering the assessment for a child with a disability in your classroom?*

for children with disabilities in their classrooms. For every teacher participant, one observation session was done on a Monday morning, and one on a Tuesday afternoon. Each session lasted for three hours. Two different time frames were involved in the observations —morning and afternoon— primarily because different sets of subjects were being taught in each slot. Worksheets were used to record relevant instances in the classroom in relation to assessment strategies. After that, the interviews took place (usually on a Wednesday), and after the interviews, two more observation sessions were carried out per teacher, one on a Thursday morning, and another on a Friday afternoon. Hence 2 interviews and 4 observation sessions were carried out per teacher, i.e. 12 observations and 6 qualitative interviews in total.

4.3.3 Data Analysis

The data collected from interviews and observations were analysed through the constructivist procedure suggested by Marshall and Rossman (2011), which has several phases. First, we organised the data by listing it on note cards, performing the minor editing necessary to make field-notes retrievable, and transcribing the interviews verbatim. In the second phase, we immersed ourselves in the data by taking the time to read and reread them several times which helped us become familiar with the material as per Marshall and Rossman's (2011) suggestion: 'researchers should think of data as something to cuddle up with, embrace, and get to know better' (p. 210). In the third stage, we generated categories and themes from the data using the two sub-questions of the study. The first sub-question provided categories regarding the types of assessment and it further provided themes on specific assessment strategies that teachers used under each assessment type. The second sub-question created categories on content and delivery of assessment strategies, and each category led to the development of specific themes such as proximity, use of technology, and length and content of assessment strategies. In the fourth stage, from the generated categories and themes, we started coding the data by using both the readings of the data, and the conceptual framework provided in the literature in relation to assessment, in order for us to see how the data on assessment strategies function or nest in their context and what varieties appear and how frequently the different varieties appear. In the fifth stage, we provided interpretations of the coded data. In this phase, we brought meaning and coherence to the themes, patterns, and categories, developed linkages and a story line related to assessment strategies that made sense and was engaging to read. Part of this phase was concerned with evaluating the data for their usefulness and centrality. In the sixth and final stage, the searching for alternative understandings took place with us constantly evaluating the plausibility of our developing understandings on the data regarding assessment strategies to ensure the quality and credibility of the study. Finally, this phase framed the writing of the final report by helping us summarise and reflect on the complexity of the findings.

4.3.4   *Trustworthiness*

In constructivist qualitative studies, validity is usually referred to as *trustworthiness* (Davies & Dodd, 2002; Mishler, 2000; Stenbacka, 2001). In our study, we explored the concept by considering two criteria commonly used for this purpose by qualitative researchers, namely, *credibility* and *transferability*.

The credibility of this study was ensured with the use of the following processes: firstly, we used *triangulation*, the process of utilising different methods when collecting data (Punch, 2009), and accordingly we employed two data collection methods, namely, semi-structured interviews and direct observations. Secondly, we used *iterative questioning*, which allowed us to detect any contradictions that emerged in participants' statements. Finally, we used *member checking*, a process according to which the researcher asks participants whether the collected data are correct (Shenton, 2004). Each participant was sent the transcript of their interview and this allowed us to get the reactions, corrections, and further insights of the participants about the interview data.

Patton (2002) emphasises that *transferability* or external validity, 'is concerned with the extent to which the findings of one study can be applied to other situations' (p. 22). Since the findings of this qualitative study were specific to a small number of individuals and contexts, it seems impossible to demonstrate that the findings and conclusions are applicable to other situations and populations. However, it is argued that the prospect of transferability should not be immediately rejected especially in research projects that utilise *multiple environments* (Brewer & Hunter, 1999). It is useful to note again here that this study involved three teachers coming from three different mainstream primary schools in the province of Negros Oriental. These schools were located in different regions within the province, which we argue qualify as *multiple environments* and therefore, our study fulfils partially the transferability requirement of a qualitative study.

We also recognised from the outset the threats to our study's credibility and transferability. One of which was researcher bias due to the social interaction component of the interviewer-interviewee relationship. Kvale and Brinkmann (2009) describe it as 'the asymmetrical power relations of the research interviewer and the interviewed subject'. In response to this threat, we had to reflect on our status and position as researchers. The first author had worked closely with all three participants over three years in the past on an inclusive education project. We saw that this might have motivated the participants to want to make things seem better, or to please the researcher by responding in the way that they believed he expected. To minimise this risk, we made sure that the participants were clear on the nature of research (Field & Morse, 1995), and stressed the fact that we were absolutely not collecting data for evaluation purposes. We did this at the orientation activity with participants before the research commenced and before the interviews were conducted. In continuously reflecting on our researcher status and its impact on our findings, we followed Field and Morse's suggestion:

> The researchers [...] should examine and declare their underlying values and assumptions in light of the research situation so that they can be considered when reading the research. (1995: p. 56)

4.4   FINDINGS

Based on the research sub-questions, the findings were organised in two main themes, namely, *types of assessment strategies* and *delivery of assessment strategies* (see Table 4.2 for a summary of all themes and sub-themes that emerged from the analysis).

4.4.1   Types of Assessment Strategies

The three teachers interviewed showed a substantial understanding of the concept of *assessment* and its importance for children with disabilities. This was manifested when they were able to categorise assessment strategies as

Table 4.2   Themes and sub-themes emerging from the data

Themes	1.	Types of assessment strategies	2.	Delivery of assessment strategies
Subthemes	1.1.	Diagnostic assessment	2.1.	Assessment content
	1.1.1.	Tests	2.1.1.	Use of native language
	1.1.2.	Informal observations	2.1.2.	Adjustment of level of difficulty
	1.1.3.	Previous teacher recommendations	2.1.3.	Adjustment of length
	1.2.	Formative assessment	2.2.	Assessment delivery
	1.2.1.	Individual work	2.2.1.	Proximity
	1.2.2.	Paired work	2.2.2.	Peer support
	1.2.3.	Group work	2.2.3.	Use of technology
			2.2.4.	Time element
	1.3.	Summative assessment		
	1.3.1.	Tests		
	1.3.2.	Group work activities		
	1.3.3.	Portfolios		

diagnostic, formative, and summative. We can argue that this level of awareness is context specific, and a result of how assessment is explicitly emphasised especially in certain education policies in the Philippines. This relates to the perspectives of *equity* and *personal fulfilment and satisfaction*. Recognising that assessment is not merely a 'summative' tool is a manifestation that teachers are sensitive towards the diversity children may bring in the classrooms. This emphasises that assessment should be utilised as an opportunity to promote equity and learning within the education system, and not as a way of 'judging' children. In addition, the teachers' use of formative assessment, for example, exemplifies the idea of *learner-centeredness* within the perspective of *personal fulfilment and satisfaction* and the teachers said that they took the time out to substantially monitor how the children were performing during instruction. This allowed teachers to make necessary adjustments or improvements in the teaching and learning process.

According to the interviews, the teachers used specific assessment strategies per assessment function in their classrooms. These specific assessment strategies came in varied forms to ensure that children with disabilities had more options to express their learning in class. This is strongly linked to the concept of *dynamic assessment* primarily because of the fact that teachers go beyond using 'pen and paper' tests, which are characterised as static testing. The use of groupings, for example, reflects the characteristics of dynamic assessment as being 'interactive, open ended, and generate information about the responsiveness of the learner to intervention' (Lidz & Elliot, 2005: p. 103). Furthermore, it is important to note that the application of the principles of dynamic assessment is not solely related to the teachers' use of varied assessment strategies; it is also significantly linked to how they deliver them to children with disabilities.

Overall, teachers' awareness and use of varied assessment strategies reflects that they were sensitive to the needs of children with disabilities. They moreover followed the guidelines given by the Department of Education especially regarding the use of 'pen and paper tests' in diagnostic and summative assessments. However, it is important to highlight that there were certain assessment strategies that teachers employed that are not necessarily mandated by the Department of Education. These include the use of observations with anecdotal records in diagnostic assessment, and groupings in both formative and summative assessments. The next sections discuss in depth the main types of assessment that were mentioned by the teachers.

Diagnostic Assessment Strategies

Popham (2008) defines diagnostic assessment as an attempt to quantify what students already know. The teachers we interviewed emphasised that diagnostic assessment played an important role in identifying the strengths and weaknesses of children with disabilities before teaching them. In addition, our observations showed that it could also be used during lesson time, such as for example by this teacher, who said that she kept informal observation notes during her daily lessons:

> What I usually do is that I have one notebook for one child that I'd like to observe. Every time I get to see relevant behaviours, I write them down. If the behaviour becomes recurring and problematic, I make recommendations on how to address it.

It is interesting to note that the whole idea of diagnostic assessment reflects the fact that assessment should be an integral element of the Individual Education Plan (IEP) process. This means that whatever data teachers collect from diagnostic assessment should be used as the basis for creating an IEP relevant to the needs of the child with disabilities in question. However, in this study, teachers did not mention IEPs and we assume that this is because IEP is a concept that is only used among special education teachers in the Philippines. Another likely explanation is that an IEP is a document that takes time to prepare and teachers in primary schools face daily time constraints due to their numerous other responsibilities.

Within diagnostic assessment, teachers used three specific assessment strategies: (1) tests, (2) informal observations, and (3) formal recommendations from previous teachers. The tests were 'pen and paper' tests, where children with disabilities were asked to respond to given tasks in writing, and we discuss the inclusiveness or not of these tests later in this section. Informal observations were carried out by the teachers in order to gather information about how children with disabilities were performing academically and socially, while the formal recommendations from previous teachers contained critical information as to how children had performed in the previous year and how the current teachers could accommodate them in specific aspects or areas of learning. One teacher reflected on the benefits of this approach:

> The good thing about having recommendation documents is that I can always approach the previous grade level teacher to clarify some important

things presented in the documents. I always find time to talk with the teacher so that I will get a clear idea on how I can teach the child best. This encourages cooperation between us, teachers.

The tests used as a diagnostic tool by teachers in this study were administered twice, i.e. pre and a post learning. This process is strongly linked to the 'sandwich' design of dynamic assessment, which implies that before an instruction, a child with a disability is given a pre-test to identify his or her strengths. Instruction then follows. The child's learning is finally assessed based on a post-test. All teachers described this process as follows: they administered a pre-test at the start of the school year and used the results of the test to support instruction. Post-test then followed in the form of periodical tests.

Tests should not solely be used to diagnose children's strengths and weaknesses primarily because they do not holistically capture the strengths and weaknesses of children with disabilities. For example, a test that requires reading and writing skills might not be accessible to a child with dyslexia or with a visual impairment (Carney & Sheppard, 2003; Handler & Fierson, 2011). This is why teachers of children with disabilities need to explore other strategies of determining the strengths and weaknesses of these children before teaching them. Therefore, it is important that the teachers in this study made use of the recommendations made by the previous year's teachers and informal observations on a daily basis to complement the results of the 'pen and paper' diagnostic tests. It is also relevant to mention that teachers took the time necessary to approach the previous teachers and discuss further their recommendations, which can be a challenge given that this time is not timetabled into their daily routines.

Formative Assessment Strategies
In relation to formative assessment, which seeks to determine how students are progressing through a certain learning goal (Wininger, 2005), the following strategies were used by the teachers: (1) individual work, (2) paired work, and (3) group work. These strategies require different mechanisms, but focus on a similar purpose, according to the teachers themselves, i.e. to inform instruction. This practice seemed to reflect the teachers' awareness and sensitivity towards the diverse needs of children with disabilities in their classrooms.

The individual work was similar to a self-assessment strategy in that it utilised journal writing, for example, to allow children to express their reflections. As exemplified in the literature, journal writing is a common strategy in assessing children with disabilities. This was specifically manifested in two empirical studies done by Brady and Kennedy (2011) and McMiller (2010) stressing that assessment should be a formative process and a demonstration of real achievement.

The use of 'Think Pair Share' as a specific activity in pairs in formative assessment brings Zone of Proximal Development (ZPD) (Chaiklin, 2003) and mediated learning experiences into the picture. This is due to the fact that according to the teachers, the main purpose of employing paired work activities was to allow a more competent child to work with a child with a disability in order to accomplish a task. Furthermore, this was to encourage a child with a disability to work with the help or support from someone in class. The Zone of Proximal Development and mediated learning experiences are relevant here because the child is provided with the so-called 'scaffolding' in the form of human assistance or support.

The group work activities employed by the teachers in this study were strongly linked to the principles of differentiated instruction and flexible groupings during assessment. Tomlinson (2001) argues that the use of differentiated outputs for certain tasks is an essential aspect of tailoring the assessment to meet individual needs. In this study, differentiated outputs took the forms of drawing, role-playing, diagramming, and other creative activities. These forms were based on student readiness, interest, or learning profile as reflected in the principles of differentiated instruction. However, it is important to stress that the employment of group work activities may pose a challenge in the classroom. In most cases, in the Philippines, one teacher has more than 50 children in a small classroom and doing flexible groupings may impose further challenges on classroom management and time. We would like to stress that good planning is essential before using such activities in the classroom to ensure their smooth and meaningful implementation. In this study, the teachers did come from government primary schools where they had an average number of 40 children per class. However, they were able to use differentiation to some extent and to make varied formative assessment strategies a natural part of their daily lessons as much as possible.

Summative Assessment Strategies

Aside from diagnostic and formative assessment strategies, the teachers also made use of varied strategies of summative assessment, a process, which assesses students' mastery of a topic after instruction (Black &

Wiliam, 2003). In the context of this study, the summative assessment strategies were divided into: (1) tests, (2) performance, and (3) product assessments (Brady & Kennedy, 2003). The weekly quizzes and periodical tests fall under tests, while group work activities and portfolios were examples of performance assessment and product assessment, respectively. However, tests were consistently used as the main summative assessment strategy. Tests are considered as a form of traditional assessment and are explicitly highlighted in the K to 12 Basic Education Curriculum. In other words, tests are standardised tools that teachers have to use when assessing children.

However, as we mentioned before, since tests are generally in a 'pen and paper' format, where children are required to respond to questions or tasks in writing, tests have the potential to exclude children with disabilities, especially those with reading and writing difficulties. Consequently tests should not be used as the only summative assessment strategy and there is a big need for teachers to look for other strategies that match the needs of children with disabilities. This was reflected by the experiences of the teachers in the study. Two of them used other summative assessment strategies for children with disabilities, namely, portfolios and group work activities with the use of checklists and rating scales. One teacher explained the rationale for this approach:

> I do not think it is fair to assess the learning of the child just through pen and paper tests. What if the child has other ways of expressing what he or she knows, not necessarily through writing? It is in that reason that as a teacher, I am looking for another strategy that is responsive to the needs of the child. And to be specific, I use portfolios.

Literature highlights the benefits of portfolios (Brady & Kennedy, 2003) because of their features that allow students some degree of choice of entries such as drawing, essays, diagrams, and art works. On the other hand, the use of group work activities with varied outputs allows the students to demonstrate their learning based on their interests or readiness, which is a key characteristic of differentiated learning as mentioned before.

4.4.2 Delivery of Assessment Strategies

How the teachers in this study delivered the various assessment strategies to children with disabilities again demonstrated their sensitivity towards the needs of these children. Instead of sticking to the traditional means of delivering assessments, they took the time out to differentiate and to develop innovative strategies so that the children would be able to give appropriate responses to given tasks. Several empirical studies (e.g. Brady & Kennedy, 2011; McMiller, 2010; Taylor, 2009) suggest that teachers play a critical role in making the classroom atmosphere responsive and relevant to the needs of children with disabilities. This includes how teachers differentiate their instructional practices, part of which is the assessment process. In relation to differentiating instructional practices, the teachers related their assessment practices to the concept of *differentiated instruction*, which strongly suggests that certain aspects of teaching have to be considered when dealing with diversity, namely, content, process, products, and learning environment. This was manifested by how the teachers continuously considered assessment *content* and *delivery* for those children with disabilities, as we demonstrate in the following sections.

Assessment Content

In terms of assessment content, the use of a child's native *language* in the assessment process was identified as one important strategy. We would like to stress that this practice, in the Philippine context, is believed to enhance learning as exemplified in the K to 12 Basic Education Programme. The rationale behind this is based on strong theoretical justifications that the children learn best through their native language (King & Mackey, 2007; Kosonen, 2005; Malone, 2003). Delivering the assessment to children in their native language allows them to fully grasp the task and provide appropriate responses. This view is strongly linked with one of the principles of dynamic assessment, as stated by Kozulin (2001): 'cognitive processes are modifiable, and an important task of assessment is to ascertain their degree of modifiability, rather than to remain limited to estimation of the child's manifest level of functioning' (p. 23).

Also related to assessment content was the teachers' strategy to adjust the *level of difficulty* and *length* of their assessments for children with disabilities. This was manifested in the fact that if teachers, for example, sensed that children with disabilities were not ready for the level of difficulty of a given assessment, they had to simplify it in order to meet the needs of the children. This is primarily because of the fact that some children may have partial mastery of the content or display mistaken ideas about the content (Tomlinson, 2001). Finally, modifying the length of the assessment, especially shortening it, was one consideration that teachers in our study made under the content of differentiated instruction (Hall, 2002) as a teacher put it:

> For weekly quizzes, I usually shorten the items for [name of child]. This is primarily because he easily loses his attention and focus in doing long tests. So instead of taking a 20-item test, I would give him a 7–10-item one.

Assessment Delivery

Four essential categories were identified in under the sub-theme 'assessment delivery', namely, (1) proximity, (2) peer support, (3) use of technology, and (4) time element. According to the teachers, these played an important role in ensuring that children with disabilities were able to effectively demonstrate their learning using varied means of assessment delivery.

As mentioned before, *proximity* and *peer support* as assessment delivery strategies are linked with the Zone of Proximal Development (ZPD) through its mediated learning experiences component. The teachers' purpose of employing these two strategies was to provide assistance to children with disabilities so that they would be able to accomplish certain assessment tasks. This matches what mediated learning experiences are all about—they occur when a more skilled adult like a teacher assists the child to do something that he or she could not do independently. However, it is useful to stress that the employment of mediated learning experiences requires a lot of skill on the part of the teacher in order to ensure that a child will not become too dependent on the teacher. This is where *fading* comes in, a process involving the gradual removal of assistance given by the skilled person to the child, and this was explicitly seen during the class observations in this study.

However, in the Philippine context where teachers teach in large classes, *proximity* can be time consuming and can put too much pressure on the teachers. This is the reason, according to the teachers, why the idea of *peer support* was developed with the aim of utilising the potential of the peers as partners. In the literature there is evidence for the benefits of peer support or the involvement of more learners when scaffolding tasks. For example, Tolmie et al. (2005) showed that scaffolding threesomes for learning tasks produced better outcomes than one-to-one when the tutor focused on the basic task, using group discussion. Moreover, Howe and

Tolmie (2003) in their research on scaffolding foursomes for controlled experiments in primary science lessons demonstrated that scaffolding is effective if the group have an opportunity to first produce a common understanding of the task. Another very important outcome of collaborative learning are its social benefits, namely, the development of social skills of the children involved (see Tolmie et al., 2010).

The assistance teachers gave to children with disabilities in relation to assessment in this study was also translated in *use of technology*. In this context, technology took the form of low-tech materials that were readily available for teachers to use. In the assessment process, both low-tech (that refers to simple technology, often of a traditional or non-mechanical kind) and high-tech (that refers to the most advanced technology available) resources play an important role in ensuring that children receive support that allows them to accomplish tasks. Although in the Philippine context, high-tech becomes more and more available, there are still instances when schools do not have the luxury of accessing it. This results in teachers only adapting existing resources as seen in the practices of teachers in this study:

> In making a test for a child with a disability, I always make sure that it does not overwhelm him because it has a lot of texts or the fonts are too small or the spacing is problematic. The test paper itself has to be responsive to the needs of the child.

Finally, it is important to highlight that one strategy for assessment delivery in relation to children with disabilities was the *time element*. This practice reflected the reality that when teachers gave children with disabilities a particular task, the latter needed more time to accomplish it. As shared by one teacher:

> Adjusting the time is very important for [name of child] primarily because of the fact that he does have intellectual limitations. I want him to have more time so that he will be able to give his best in answering the test.

Time element is a critical element exemplified in the process of differentiation. Tomlinson (2001) asserts that when teachers deal with the diverse needs of the children in the classroom, the instruction or assessment process has to be differentiated either through flexible groupings or time extension. This strategy allows children to give appropriate responses to the given tasks.

4.5 Moving Forward: Possibilities and Challenges

The purpose of conducting this qualitative study was to explore how primary school teachers assessed children with disabilities in mainstream classrooms in a province of the Philippines. The ultimate aim was to contribute to the moving forward of inclusive education in the Philippines. As we noted in the introductory sections, although certain efforts or initiatives on inclusive education have been implemented in the province of Negros Oriental, there seems to be a lack of empirical studies documenting them. The findings of the study presented in this chapter are helpful in moving forward the assessment of children with disabilities in several ways.

Firstly, there was a strong connection between theoretical perspectives on assessment (such as ZPD and mediated learning experience) and the practices of teachers interviewed for this study. We assume that this may be due to the fact that these theoretical perspectives became the basis of education policies related to assessment in the Philippines specifically the K to 12 Basic Education Programme; and policies need to be translated into classroom practices. However, it must be noted that although certain assessment strategies such as tests are a requirement that teachers should practice in the classroom, it seemed that many other strategies used by the teachers in this study were the products of the teachers' own efforts and exploration, at the expense of their personal time. Moreover, the findings of this study provide an important lesson to teachers that in assessing children with disabilities, employment of variety of strategies is a necessity. Sticking to traditional methods without exploring other strategies does not help respond to the diverse needs of children with disabilities. Hence it is important to emphasise that how the teachers assessed children with disabilities demonstrated innovation, creativity, and willingness which are all important ingredients of inclusive education, especially in challenged contexts like the Philippines. This scenario again highlights the teachers' role in the successful inclusion of children with disabilities.

Secondly, this study provided a unique opportunity to listen to the voices of teachers from a small locality in moving towards inclusive education. Interviewing the three teachers in this study created a space for them to share their experiences of assessing children with disabilities. In sharing their experiences, they illustrated many examples of good practice, but also many gaps in terms of the support they receive when implementing inclusive education. We recommend that these voices become an integral part of decision- and policy-making processes. It is high time to close the gap between policy and practice by creating an education system that gives central importance to the voices and experiences of teachers through more studies like ours that will eventually help map current successful practices, identify problems, and create a pool of practice-based evidence.

Thirdly, although it appeared that teachers in this study had a substantial level of awareness of assessment as a concept, we were left with unanswered questions regarding the use of Individualized Education Plans (IEPs) in the process of assessment. We recognise that due to its small sample, our study's findings may have limited generalisability. However, it is useful to note here that the special and inclusive education literature praises the merits of the IEP in the teaching of children with disabilities. In this study, IEP was not a part of the assessment practices of teachers. Taylor (2009) maintains that this happens especially when teachers do not have the capacity to execute the plan because of a handful of other responsibilities that are part of their daily role. Although the mentioned reasons can be regarded as valid, we argue that the value of an IEP should not be underestimated and that efforts are needed to recondsider its use in practice. In addition, it is useful to remind ourselves that differentiating assessment is not only applicable to children with disabilities. Due to the increasing diversity of learners in mainstream classrooms, differentiation has to be employed not only for the selected few but for all learners.

Finally, we recognise that this study has limitations, which can be addressed by future studies. For example, this study had a very wide focus on the types of disability and subject areas. We think that in the future studies, researchers could focus on one specific type of disability and how assessment strategies in the Philippines are used in response to this type of disability. For example, the assessment strategies suitable for a child within the Autistic Spectrum may not necessarily be the same with those that would be beneficial for a child with a Visual Impairment. In addition, we also recommend that specific subject areas are considered in relation to assessment strategies. This means that future researchers could explore, for example, the assessment strategies suitable for a child with dyslexia across different subjects.

In closing, we would like to emphasise that in moving towards inclusive education, the whole education community must strive to explore the perspectives of 'global South' contexts like the Philippines. In contexts where resources are a huge challenge due to poverty, the implementation of inclusive education becomes a herculean effort. It is therefore empowering to note that amidst this hard reality, our study captured instances where inclusive teaching and learning does happen, and this seemed to be thanks to the efforts of dedicated and committed teachers, who are at the forefront of the realisation of inclusive education.

REFERENCES

Baessa, Y. (2008). Research in a developing country. *American Psychological Association, 12*(2), 2–15.

Black, P., & William, D. (2003). In praise of educational research: Formative assessment. *British Educational Research Journal, 29*(5), 623–637.

Brady, L., & Kennedy, K. (2003). *Celebrating student achievement: Assessment and reporting.* Australia: Pearson Education.

Brady, L., & Kennedy, K. (2011). *Assessment and reporting: Celebrating student achievement* (4th ed.). Australia: Pearson Education.

Brewer, J., & Hunter, A. (1999). *Multimethod research: A synthesis of styles* (3rd ed.). Newbury Park: Sage.

Carney, S., & Sheppard, V. (2003). *Teaching students with visual impairments.* Saskatchewan: Saskatchewan Learning.

Chaiklin, S. (2003). *The zone of proximal development in Vygotsky's analysis of learning and instruction.* Cambridge: University Press.

Charmaz, K. (2006). *Objectivist and constructivist methods of research.* Thousand Oaks: Sage.

Cohen, L., Manion, L., & Morrison, K. (Eds.). (2007). *Research methods in education* (6th ed.). London: Routledge.

Corbin, J., & Strauss, A. (2008). *Basics of qualitative research: Techniques and procedures for developing grounded theory.* London: Sage.

Creswell, J. W. (2007). *Designing a qualitative study: Choosing among five approaches* (2nd ed.). Thousand Oaks: Sage.

Davies, D., & Dodd, J. (2002). Qualitative research and the question of rigor. *Qualitative Research, 12*(2), 279–289.

Department of Education. (2012). *The Philippine education system.* Manila: DepEd.

Department of Education. (2015). *Republic of the Philippines: Department of education.* Manila: DepEd.

Field, P. A., & Morse, J. M. (1995). *Research: Application of qualitative approaches.* Kent: Croom Helm.

GPRehab. (2013). *Plight of children with disabilities in education in Negros Oriental.* Negros Oriental: GPRehab.

Hall, T. (2002). *Differentiated instruction.* Wakefield: National Center on Accessing the General Curriculum.

Handler, S. M., & Fierson, W. M. (2011). Learning disabilities, dyslexia, and vision. *Pediatrics, 127*(3), 23–36.

Howe, C. J., & Tolmie, A. (2003). Group work in primary school science: Discussion, consensus and guidance from experts. *International Journal of Educational Research, 39*, 51–72.

King, K., & Mackey, A. (2007). *The bilingual edge: Why, when, and how to teach your child a second language.* New York: Collins.

Kosonen, K. (2005). Education in local languages: Policy and practice in Southeast Asia. In *First languages first: Community-based literacy programmes for minority language contexts in Asia.* Bangkok: UNESCO Bangkok.

Kozulin, A. (2001). Psychological tools and mediated learning. In A. Kozulin, B. Gindis, V. Ageyev, & S. Miller (Eds.), *Vygotsky's educational theory in cultural context* (pp. 15–38). Cambridge: University Press.

Kvale, S., & Brinkmann, S. (2009). *InterViews: Learning the craft of qualitative research interviewing* (2nd ed.). Thousand Oaks: Sage.

Lidz, C., & Elliott, J. (Eds.). (2005). *Dynamic assessment: Prevailing models and applications.* Amsterdam: Elsevier Science.

Ma, J. (2013, June 16). The heart of an inclusive teacher. *The Advocate, 22*, 6.

Malone, D. L. (2003). Developing curriculum materials for endangered language education: Lessons from the field. *International Journal of Bilingual Education and Bilingualism, 6*(5), 332.

Marshall, C., & Rossman, G. B. (2011). *Designing qualitative research* (5th ed.). London: Sage.

McMiller, T. S. (2010). Assessment as demonstration of real achievement. *International Journal on Inclusive Education, 10*(1), 115–131.

Mertens, D. M. (2005). *Research methods in education and psychology: Integrating diversity with quantitative and qualitative approaches* (2nd ed.). Thousand Oaks: Sage.

Miles, S., & Singal, N. (2010). Education for all and inclusive education debate: Conflict, contradiction, or opportunity? *International Journal of Inclusive Education, 14*(1), 14–15.

Mishler, E. G. (2000). Validation in inquiry-guided research: The role of exemplars. In B. M. Verzuela, J. P. Stewart, R. G. Carillo, & J. G. Berger (Eds.), *Acts of inquiry in qualitative research* (pp. 119–146). Cambridge: Harvard Educational Review.

Patton, M. Q. (2002). *Qualitative research and evaluation methods* (3rd ed.). Thousand Oaks: Sage.

Popham, W. J. (2008). *Transformative assessment.* Alexandria: Association for Supervision and Curriculum Development.

Punch, K. F. (2009). *Introduction to research methods in education.* London: Sage.

SEAMEO & INNOTECH. (2012). *K to 12 toolkit.* Manila: SEAMEO & INNOTECH. Retrieved form http://www.gov.ph/downloads/2012/201209-K-to-12-Toolkit.pdf

Shenton, A. K. (2004). Strategies for ensuring trustworthiness in qualitative research projects. *Education for Information, 22*, 63–75.

Stenbacka, C. (2001). Quality research requires quality concepts of its own. *Management Decision, 39*(7), 351–355.

Taylor, R. L. (2009). IEP and the assessment of exceptional students. *International Journal of Inclusive Education, 22*(11), 238–272.

Tolmie, A., Thomson, J. A., Foot, H. C., Whelan, K., Morrison, S., & McLaren, B. (2005). The effects of adult guidance and peer discussion on the development of children's representations: Evidence from the training of pedestrian skills. *British Journal of Psychology, 96*, 181–204.

Tolmie, A. K., Topping, K. J., Christie, D., Donaldson, C., Howe, C., Jessiman, E., et al. (2010). Social effects of collaborative learning in primary schools. *Learning and Instruction, 20*, 177–191.

Tomlinson, C. A. (2001). *How to differentiate instruction in mixed ability classrooms* (2nd ed.). Alexandria: Association for Supervision and Curriculum Development.

UNESCO. (2015). *The Philippine case study*. Philippines: UNESCO.

Wininger, R. S. (2005). Using your tests to teach: Formative summative assessment. *Teaching Psychology, 32*(2), 164–166.

Woods, P., & Pratt, N. (2006). *Qualitative research*. London: Open University Press.

Fig. 5.1 Map of Belize (Source: http://www.d-maps.com/m/america/belize/belize22.gif)

CHAPTER 5

The Perspectives of Teachers in Belize in Relation to Working with Visually Impaired Pupils in Mainstream Schools: An Exploratory Study

Joycelyn Nair Azueta and Leda Kamenopoulou

Abstract Chapter 5 presents a research that explored the perspectives of teachers working with children with visual impairment/blindness in mainstream schools in Belize. A qualitative approach was adopted and semi-structured interviews were conducted with 8 teachers from 6 selected schools located in different regions. Findings suggest that the teachers perceived inclusion as equality of opportunity for children with disabilities and felt that inclusive education has many benefits for all children. The research also recorded numerous strategies that the teachers used with children with a visual impairment/blindness. The main challenges mentioned by teachers were the lack of training and resources. The authors conclude that teachers seemed generally supportive of inclusion of visually

J. N. Azueta (✉)
Belmopan, Belize

L. Kamenopoulou
University of Roehampton, London, UK

© The Author(s) 2018   111
L. Kamenopoulou (ed.), *Inclusive Education and Disability in the Global South*, https://doi.org/10.1007/978-3-319-72829-2_5

impaired students, but they felt they needed more specialised knowledge and support in this area.

Keywords Visual impairment • Inclusion • Teacher views • Teaching strategies • Belize

'[I]nclusion is possible with [the] right equipment, which we do not have.'
(Teacher)

5.1   INTRODUCTION

Evidence suggests that disability can increase the possibility for greater exclusion in education and this is more evident in developing countries where poverty and disability are highly correlated (see, Banks & Polack, 2014). UNESCO's past and present strategies like the Education for All, the Millennium Goals and the Sustainable Development Goals (SDGs) prioritise the provision of quality education to all children regardless of their socio-economic and cultural background, gender, race, ethnicity or disability.

Inclusive education for children with disabilities is seen as the best way of operationalising these frameworks and meeting the internationally agreed goals, particularly in developing countries such as Belize (Eklindh & Van den Brule-Balescut, 2006; Peters, 2003). Although Belize has ratified the relevant international conventions and adopted a policy for inclusive education, the unavailability of effective practices to meet the needs of some children in mainstream schools is evident across schools and districts (Young, 2012).

One of the main reasons for this is the lack of resources, particularly in the rural areas of the country where there is greater population dispersal (Young, 2012). For instance, children in rural communities have limited access to early childhood education and for those who have disabilities, receiving support from resource centres is a major challenge (UNICEF, 2012). The Convention on the Rights of the Child (CRC) states that 'all children with disabilities have the right to education, training, health care services, rehabilitation services, preparation for employment and recreational opportunities' (Owen, 2003: p. 7).

Belize has signed and ratified both the CRC and the CRPD (Convention on the Rights of Persons with Disabilities). The ratification of the CRPD was possibly one of the key milestones for increasing the disability awareness movement in Belize, because most of the provisions in this document were also included in the National Policy for Persons with Disabilities (which was drafted in 2005) and the National Plan of Action for Children (2004–2014). Unfortunately, neither of the latter legal documents has been ratified to date (UNICEF, 2012), and according to the International Disability Rights Monitor (IDRM) (2004), Belize is one of the few countries in the Caribbean with no actual legal protections for persons with disabilities.

Hence although Belize recognises the importance of safeguarding all children with the right to education and is a signatory to the international conventions, there seems to be a failure to translate these policies into law, and subsequently into successful practice. In this chapter, we present a study we conducted on the views and experiences of mainstream teachers in Belize in relation to teaching children with Visual Impairment (VI) or Blindness, thereafter called VI. We adopted a qualitative approach and carried out semi-structured interviews with 8 teachers from 6 selected schools located in different regions. Our findings suggest that teachers perceive inclusion as equality of opportunity for children with disabilities in terms of accessing mainstream schools and that inclusion has many benefits for all children. We also recorded numerous strategies that teachers use when working with children with a VI. The main challenges mentioned by teachers were lack of appropriate training and resources. We can conclude that teachers seemed overall supportive of inclusion of students with visual impairment, but they said that they needed more professional support in this area.

5.2 Inclusive and Special Education in Belize

Belize is a small country in Central America with a population of 374, 315, 57,000 of which live in Belize City (http://worldpopulationreview. com/countries/belize-population/). Belize is a vibrant multi-ethnic country with different ethnic groups, including Mestizo, Creole, Garinagu, Yucatec and Q'eqchi Maya, East Indian and small numbers of Mennonite, Asian and European immigrants. The official language is English, but Creole and Spanish are also widely used. Belize's economy relies on agriculture, marine products and also tourism and like other global South countries; it has faced challenges over the last years due to a rapidly growing population and declining markets. Education remains one of the big priorities for the Belize government (UNESCO, 2007).

In 2007, the Caribbean Symposium on Inclusive Education took place in Kingston, Jamaica, organised by UNESCO. One of the outputs of this event was the 'Belize Report on Inclusive Education' (UNESCO, 2007), which provides a lot of information on the current status, major challenges, and key priorities for inclusive education in Belize. It also provides a useful overview of the Belize education system, especially in relation to special and inclusive education, including some historical information, which we summarise here.

According to the report (UNESCO, 2007), over the past 25 years, the perception and understanding of both special and inclusive education in Belize has changed significantly. In 1991, the Special Education Unit (SEU) was established with a mission and ideas that clearly reflected the then beliefs around the education of children with disabilities. During this time, the perception of special education was based on the idea that special education was to be provided by this special unit whose operation was independent and focused on the provision of services to students with disabilities. Over the years that followed, special education in Belize ended up as an independent and autonomous sector, accomplishing its objectives without any communication with the general (i.e. mainstream) education system or other sectors of the Ministry of Education (MOE).

During this same period of the 1990's, there was the establishment of new special schools and centres, and the merging of the Lynn School for students with intellectual impairments with the Stella Maris School for students with other disabilities. Some in the education field saw these as positive steps since these special schools or units provided special education services to students with disabilities. However, as the demand for these services increased, they became more and more strained, and after international pressures for educational reform, the SEU had to evaluate its practices and work more towards collaborating with the general education system.

Therefore, in Belize special education services for children with disabilities have progressively shifted from being a separate entity to being part of the general education system. Moreover, the perception of inclusive education has gradually shifted from referring to 'provisions for children with special needs' to 'a heightened awareness of the need to ensure that no child is excluded from acquiring a basic education' (UNESCO, 2007: pp. 2–3). In other words, Belize has been and still is on a long journey from segregation and exclusion to mainstream placement of children with disabilities, and reducing exclusions and ensuring the right to basic education for all children.

5.3   EDUCATION OF VISUALLY IMPAIRED (VI) PUPILS IN BELIZE

The population of VI children in Belize is not exactly known but is estimated as being approximately evenly distributed in terms of gender across rural and urban areas of the country (Young, 2012). Currently Belize has 50 children registered blind, who attend primary and secondary mainstream schools (BCVI, 2015). In terms of the severity and cause of VI in these cases, it ranges from low vision to complete blindness, and the majority are the result of Retinopathy of Prematurity (ROP) (BCVI, 2015). Moreover, there seems to be a higher percentage of cases in rural areas compared to urban areas, possibly due to the lack of health resources. Those who only have a VI have either no vision at all or some minimal light perception or varying degrees of low vision. However, in some cases VI is accompanied by additional disabilities like a hearing impairment, in which case, the effects of multiple disabilities cause more and more complex difficulties in social interactions and within learning environments (Kamenopoulou, 2012).

Young (2012) points out that Belize has signed several international agreements that concern the education of children with disabilities including those with VI. Examples include the Salamanca Statement and Framework for Action for Special Needs Education (1994) and the Dakar Framework of Action (2000). Despite these international documents being in turn recognised in national laws, policies and action plans for the provision of quality education, the Situation Analysis of Children with Disabilities (UNICEF, 2012) indicated that there is a major lack of resources and as well as the 'will power' necessary to translate these documents into practice. Therefore, there is a major gap to be filled in achieving inclusive education for children with disabilities in Belize, including those with VI. In his analysis of the compliance of the laws in Belize with the CRC, Owen (2003) concluded:

> Unfortunately disabled children have been largely overlooked by the laws of Belize (notably no mention is made of disability in the Belize Constitution Act). (p. 7)

The Belize Council for the Visually Impaired (BCVI) provides relevant support services using a Community Based Rehabilitation (CBR) programme, which enables the families to receive the appropriate resources and services such as training and guidance of coping with a VI child at home. This support service begins once the child becomes registered with BCVI and then his or her information becomes a part of the organisation's database registry. Following this, BCVI starts to provide early stimulation to young children until they reach the age of 3 and they are ready to commence preschool. BCVI is also actively involved in providing assistance to the parents in terms of finding a suitable school placement for their child. More training continues into preschool where BCVI provides the required resources such as canes for Orientation and Mobility Skills (OMS) and Braille materials so the child can learn how to read and write in Braille. In addition to providing assistance to the VI child, BCVI goes further by providing opportunities for Braille training to teachers directly at the school or through their annual summer 'camps' for teachers (Young, 2012).

In Belize, however, there is a high possibility that only few schools have the necessary resources that would allow them to meet the needs of VI children. Many schools are governmental schools and depend on funding from the Ministry of Education (MOE) while other schools are privately operated receiving funding and donations on an ad hoc basis. Hence despite BCVIs efforts to support for teachers with some training, pure environmental factors such as lack of resources make the teaching of VI children in practice very challenging (Young, 2012).

In reality, the majority of VI students, who are placed in mainstream education classrooms, receive support from external professionals called 'itinerant teachers' or 'itinerant resource officers' (IROs). These specially trained professionals work under the National Resource Centre for Inclusive Education (NaRCIE). NaRCIE is a unit under the MOE, responsible for ensuring that the special learning needs of students are properly addressed within the existing education system in Belize. NaRCIE collaborates with other entities to promote inclusive education within the education system, and assigns IROs to each district responsible for meeting the needs of children with disabilities in mainstream schools. IROs provide screening and support services along with assistance to teachers who teach children with SEN/Disabilities. The IROs reach out to these students through referrals made by schools or parents. According to UNICEF (2012), there is a total of 11 IROs in Belize trained in special education. Although their roles and responsibilities vary in some aspects, most IROs have similar responsibilities, which include helping to identify the child's current level of performance, determining the child's needs, and setting suitable learning goals (Miles, 2003). Additionally, IROs collaborate with the mainstream education classroom teachers on curriculum adaptations and instructional modifications required based on the child's individual needs. They moreover provide direct instruction on compensatory skills (e.g., braille, listening, keyboarding); on obtaining and preparing specialised learning materials (e.g., math manipulatives); and on adapting reading assignments and text-based curriculum material into Braille or large print or audio format (Gillon & Young, 2002).

In the Belizean context, despite BCVIs efforts, training for working with VI children remains overall extremely limited. According to Young (2012) IROs are not highly skilled in braille reading and writing. According to his analysis, in 2012 there was only one IRO who was fluent in braille reading and writing and was only available in Belize City. This person was the only qualified person capable of providing training to other IROs. It can therefore be argued that a key challenge facing Belizze in the inclusion of VI pupils is the limited availability of trained persons, who can provide more training and on-going support to mainstream classroom teachers and other IROs.

5.4   Teachers' Attitudes Towards Inclusive Education

Teachers' attitudes to inclusion are crucial, because research has shown that the way teachers understand inclusion and how they feel about it is one of the factors determining its success in practice (Avramidis & Norwich, 2002; Avramidis et al., 2000).

Young (2012) reports that most teachers in Belize seem embracive of the inclusion of blind students in mainstream classrooms, but there are some who still feel that trying to meet their needs is quite challenging. In his research, he wanted to explore the situation of VI children with a focus on children and schools. Therefore, he visited the homes and schools in rural and urban areas of Belize. The schools he targeted included 10 preschools and 25 primary schools, where he interviewed VI students, their teachers, their principals, and some of their peers. In addition to home and school visits, meetings with the director from the BCVI and managers from NaRCIE were conducted to gather information on the services available for VI children in Belize. His findings revealed that some teachers do not persevere and this seems to be due to lack of relevant training. Teachers in his sample acknowledged that if provided with appropriate training, their attitudes would be more positive and their approach more successful (Young, 2012).

In the following section, we describe the methodology we adopted in order to explore in more detail the perspectives of teachers in Belize in relation to the inclusion of children with VI in their classrooms.

5.5   METHODOLOGY: APPROACH, SAMPLE AND PROCEDURES

A qualitative approach was adopted and semi-structured interviews were carried out to address the research questions. In addition, field visits with observation notes were used. There is not a single or correct way to conduct a qualitative study, and the approach lends itself to a combination of possible methods. In this case, the concepts related to the research questions (i.e. inclusive education and VI) were explored from the point of view of the teachers, who were interviewed within their natural settings (Yin, 2003). Field visits were carried out to all participating schools, including tours of the classrooms of VI students and discussions with the principals of the schools. Visits to the BCVI centre were also conducted as part of data collection. The research questions were the following:

1. How do teachers understand and feel about 'inclusion'?
2. What teaching methods/strategies do teachers use when teaching children with VI?
3. What challenges do they face when teaching children with VI?

We used a purposive sampling approach and accordingly, targeted participants and schools from across Belize. This approach allowed us to gain access to a sample of schools representative of different regions. In order to identify relevant schools, we used the database held by the BCVI, which includes a full list of schools with VI pupils and background information on the pupils and the schools. According to the database a total of 29 mainstream schools countrywide had VI students enrolled, including both primary and secondary schools. The majority of these schools were located in Belize City, and we recruited three schools from this part of the country. Two more schools were recruited from the western part of the country and one from the northern part of the country. Due to limited time and difficulties in access, no schools from the southern part were recruited. There were no schools in the Orange Walk district with VI students. In total, six schools took part in the study covering three out of the six districts of the country.

There were eight teachers in total, who agreed to participate in the interviews. Four teachers were from Belize City. Two of them were secondary school teachers and two were primary school teachers. Three participants were from the Cayo District, who were all primary school teachers and from rural villages. One teacher was a secondary teacher from an urban school in the northern part of the country.

Before commencing the interviews, which lasted up to forty minutes, participants were reminded that their participation was voluntary and reassured again that all information they provided would be kept confidential and that their identity would not be revealed in any future publication of the research findings. An interview guide was used during the interview that served as a reminder of the topics to be covered (Kvale, 1996). Each interview was audio recorded and transcribed verbatim. In the next stage, multiple readings of both transcripts and field notes were undertaken and in the final stage, data was coded using the inductive process using the research questions as the starting point for the identification and classification of relevant information. Accordingly, findings were organised into three categories: (1) teachers' perceptions of inclusion (2) teaching strategies used and (3) challenges faced.

5.6   Findings and Discussion

5.6.1   Teachers' Perceptions of Inclusion

Participants defined inclusive education as providing equal opportunities for children with disabilities to be educated alongside their normal peers. Their view was that inclusive education is giving all children an equal chance for an education. One teacher explained his idea of inclusive education:

> They will not be placed in any special environment. They will be able to sit with the regular group and more importantly, do the same activities as the regular group and be graded as the regular group. Generally, it is to have that equality.

Secondly, all participants agreed that they have a right to be placed in mainstream schools, provided the latter have the necessary resources to meet special educational needs. One participant stated:

> Lab activities in Science were extremely difficult. For lab activities, teaching the blind with inclusion is possible with right equipment, which we do not have.

Finally, all participants agreed that placing these children in mainstream schools can bring several benefits such as the development of social skills and independent life skills. This view is in agreement with arguments found in the relevant literature that inclusive education promotes educational opportunities and social development for all students, responds to diversity, stimulates understanding and tolerance and eradicates prejudice against students with disabilities (Jenkinson, 1997; Kugelmass, 2004; Peters, 2003; Rix & Simmons, 2005).

In summary, participants saw inclusive education in a positive way and believed it to be a right of all children in the name of equality of opportunity, but thought it depends on adequate resources. In other words, all eight teachers held positive attitudes towards inclusive education and argued that it is not only beneficial to the students with SEN, but also to the entire school community. This is an encouraging finding, because one of the main factors contributing to the successful implementation of any inclusive policy in schools is the positive attitude of teachers (Hodkinson, 2010). However, the teachers interviewed also clearly stated some of the barriers that they feel hamper the inclusion of VI children in practice, such as the lack of resources.

5.6.2   Teaching Methods Strategies Used to Teach VI and/or Blind Students

Participants said that they had to adapt teaching strategies in order to meet the learning needs of their VI students. In Table 5.1, we summarise all the teaching strategies that teachers mentioned, and these included audio reinforcement, Braille or tactile objects.

According to the literature, one of the main principles that underpin the adaptations made for children with VI is the use of concrete experiences

Table 5.1   Adaptive teaching strategies used by teachers

Adaptive method	Number of teachers who said they use it
Tactile and real objects	8
Audio	8
Electronic screen reader and assistive devices	2
Tutoring/extra time	3
Group discussions	8
Braille	1
Oral presentation	1

and learning primarily through the use of hearing and touch (Gallagher & Coleman, 2009). This is because often teachers must present information that typically developing children grasp through vision, and in order to make them accessible to a child with VI, teachers must plan and implement activities that will help their students acquire as much information as possible through their fully functioning senses (Salisbury, 2008). Webster and Roe (1998) also stipulate that the support teachers should provide to students with VI should be based on the use of sensory stimulation including sounds, smells, textures and shapes, for developing a better understanding of the world.

The teachers we interviewed also stressed the importance of group work and discussions, particularly in subjects such as reading, language, and history for the learning process of those students with VI. Johnsen (2001) argues that for learning to occur, an interactive process between a teacher and student in an adaptive teaching and learning environment is essential. Furthermore, Wade (2000) recommends cooperative group discussions in mainstream classrooms to discuss complex lessons and abstract concepts in order to make them more tangible.

Given the importance of using senses other than vision to convey information to and communicate with VI pupils, an interesting finding was that only one of the teachers interviewed mentioned using Braille as a strategy with those pupils. According to the BCVI (2015), teachers in Belize are not educated enough on how to use Braille materials and tactile strategies, hence they are unprepared to implement this practice, which is so crucial for the learning of children with VI, and our findings seem to confirm this situation.

5.6.3   Challenges Encountered by Teachers Who Teach VI/Blind Students

Most participants said that lack of preparation/training on sensory impairment hindered them from including students with VI in mainstream schools:

> The provision of training needs to be managed and done more efficiently. Training needs to be done in advance before the commencement of classes and continued throughout the year so as to have continuity.

BCVI (2015) also provides evidence that teachers in Belize receive only limited information about VI and this takes place in summer schools and professional development workshops that they are required to attend before the commencement of the new academic year. According to BCVI's report (2015), this is not sufficient for them to be able to work with children with special needs. Likewise, teachers in our study said they would be more open to the idea of teaching students with VI if they received proper training that will equip them with the required knowledge on special needs and more specifically sensory impairment. This finding is in line with the Belize Report on Inclusive Education (UNESCO, 2007), which sets as an immediate priority for inclusive education in Belize the adequate preparation of pre-service teachers stipulating that 'a prepared teaching force is central to the successful achievement of inclusion of all children' (p. 8).

As mentioned earlier, most participants with the exception of one, were not confident Braille users; and their VI students had little to minimal knowledge in of Braille as well. As we pointed out earlier, according to Young (2012), the IROs, who deliver teacher development workshops and training during the summer are not well versed in Braille reading or writing; and in 2012, there was only one IRO who was fluent in Braille in Belize City thus limiting the provision of training and availability of resources to urban schools and areas.

In terms of Orientation and Mobility Skills (OMS), all of the primary school teachers said their students were facing challenges in this area. They said that this was because their students had not trained during early years on how to use the cane and move in their environment, and as a result they had difficulties in moving around in the classroom and in the school; these difficulties made it really difficult for the teachers to address their needs.

I had to take him outside and show him how to get from the gate to his classroom. He had poor orientation and mobility. His feet, we had to let him do a lot of exercise because he was so dependent on his parent. So he did not have mobility at all.

Early Years Education in Belize lacks empirical research. According to the Early Childhood Development Education Officer at UNICEF in Belize City (personal communication), there is one private institution, the Inspiration Centre, currently providing training to Pre-school teachers to do early childhood intervention and assessment for children with disabilities. Furthermore, the Literacy Unit under the MOE is working on conducting screening and diagnostic tests, particularly literacy screening (Young, 2012).

Finally, teachers mentioned lack of parental involvement as one of the challenges they face when teaching children with VI.

There was no parental involvement. The mother was a single mother and had lots of children.

Studies conducted in Spain and New Brunswick reported that parents had the notion that education is clearly the responsibility of teachers (Mitchell, 2008; Simon, Echeita, Sandoval, & Lopez, 2010). There is currently a lot of debate internationally around the role of parental involvement in a child's educational attainment. For example, the next Global Education Monitoring Report is focused on accountability in education and explores who is responsible for providing children with quality education, but this issue becomes more relevant when the child has a disability, in this case VI. For example lack of parental involvement and insufficient communication with the school result in a lot of crucial information about the child not being shared with the teacher (Johnsen, 2001; Smidt, 2009). It is very important that the teachers of students with VI become familiar with details of the child's personal and educational history, such as how the loss in vision occurred and how affects the student in their learning on a daily basis (Sacks & Silberman, 1998). As a result of lack of parental involvement, teachers do what they can without being able to fully understand their students' needs or to explore how they can best teach them and help them participate in mainstream classrooms. Moreover, due to possible lack of parental stimulation at early stages of life, children come to school having missed certain experiences

Table 5.2 Challenges mentioned by teachers in relation to teaching VI/blind children

1. Lack of knowledge/training on SEN
2. Little to no knowledge of Braille
3. Low number of itinerant resource officers and lack of assistant/special needs teachers
4. Poor orientation and mobility skills of students
5. Lack of parental involvement

and lagging behind in developmental stages. For example, if not actively encouraged and supported by the parents during the early years, a child may not feel confident enough to move around and explore their environment thus resulting in poor OMS (Gallagher & Coleman, 2009). In Table 5.2 we summarise all challenges in relation to teaching VI children in mainstream classrooms that were mentioned by the 8 teachers we interviewed.

5.7   CONCLUSIONS AND RECOMMENDATIONS

Our aim was to explore Belize teachers' perspectives on the inclusion of VI students in mainstream classrooms. Under this key objective, we examined three areas, i.e. teachers' understanding of and feelings towards the inclusion of this group of children, the strategies they use to support VI pupils in their classrooms, and the challenges they encounter when teaching these children in the mainstream. Our findings suggested that teachers held mostly positive views about inclusion and believed that having these children placed in a mainstream setting brought many benefits for them in areas of social development and independent life skills; and also benefited their peers.

However, our findings also revealed that teachers thought they lacked training and resources necessary for working with this group of pupils. The need for training in Braille and adaptive strategies emerged as very important from their interviews. Overall, teachers told us that they used general teaching strategies and where possible, they made the necessary adaptations such as reinforcement of sensory stimulation through the other senses and the use of objects. The most popular methods were found to be audio and tactile ones, because participants were most comfortable with these. Moreover, we found that the eight teachers' thought that their views towards the inclusion of children with VI in schools were influenced by this lack of training and resources, and they argued that they would be more pro inclusion if they had received suitable training. Other challenges they mentioned were the lack of parental involvement and children's difficulties with OMS.

This was a very small-scale qualitative research and the above findings cannot be used to make general statements about all schools and all teaches across Belize. However, we argue that these findings provide a valuable insight into some of the local teachers' views and experiences. Based on the above findings, our recommendations are as follows:

- *Increase and improve provision for teacher training*

  Teachers expressed clearly that inclusion of VI children can be successful, but the right amount of knowledge and skills are required of the teachers, and these can only be obtained with appropriate and adequate training and continuing professional development. Hence we recommend that in Belize a more solid structure needs to be put in place for teachers and teaching professionals to be able to gain access to suitable training opportunities and relevant qualifications. The need to adequately prepare teachers prior to commencing their teaching career, as well as the need to provide on-going support for them throughout their every day practice cannot be overemphasised.

- *Provide adequate resources*

  The lack of teaching and learning resources and materials suitable for VI pupils emerged as a major challenge in the implementation of inclusive education for these teachers. It follows that the government should prioritise as much as possible the provision of enough suitable resources for schools that have VI pupils enrolled. The UNESCO (2007) report noted that big progress has taken place in Belize in this area, with funding invested for education currently being the second largest in the Belize national budget, but it seems to be the case that more concentrated efforts are needed so that teachers and pupils with special educational needs have access to necessary equipment and specialised resources.

- *Improve early assessment and intervention*

  The Government should set up and deliver disability and inclusive education awareness training to professionals including doctors and teachers, as well as parents in order to support early identification and the development of joint intervention plans from the Health, Education and Social Services sectors. More centres providing training to pre-school teachers on early assessment and intervention are needed and the MOE needs to develop an approach for including children with disabilities in mainstream classrooms that is founded on a solid and well-organised early years framework.

- *Increase parental involvement*
  The teachers we interviewed saw parental involvement as necessary support for both the child and the teacher but at the same time they said that parental engagement was an on-going challenge. Based on this, we argue that parents could also be included in training seminars that will provide them with relevant knowledge from the outset such as coping with their children's disability and communicating the needs of their child to teachers and school.

To sum up, in this chapter we presented a research exploring eight Belizean teachers' views about the inclusion of VI pupils in their classrooms, including their perceptions of inclusion, the strategies they use and the challenges they face when working with these children. Based on our findings, we provided specific recommendations that will hopefully help move forward the implementation of inclusive education in a country that still has a lot of work to do in this area. We hope that our study will open the doors to future researchers interested in exploring inclusive education in Belize in more breadth and depth.

REFERENCES

Avramidis, E., Bayliss, P., & Burden, R. (2000). A survey into mainstream teachers' attitudes towards the inclusion of children with special educational needs in the ordinary school in one local education authority. *Educational Psychology, 20*(2), 191–211.

Avramidis, E., & Norwich, B. (2002). Teachers' attitudes towards integration/inclusion: A review of the literature. *European Journal of Special Needs Education, 17*(2), 129–147.

Banks, L. M., & Polack, S. (2014). *The economic costs of exclusion and gains of inclusion of people with disabilities*. London: CBM/International Centre for Evidence in Disability, London School of Hygiene and Tropical Medicine.

Belize Council for the Visually Impaired (BCVI). (2015). *Annual reports 2002–2015*. Belize: BCVI.

Belize population, in World Population Overview (n.d.). Retrieved May 19, 2017, from http://worldpopulationreview.com/countries/belize-population/

Eklindh, K., & Van den Brule-Balescut, J. (2006). The right to education for persons with disabilities: Reflecting on UNESCO's role from Salamanca to the convention on the rights of persons with disabilities. In H. Savolainen, M. Matero, & H. Kokkala (Eds.), *When all means all: Experiences in three African countries with EFA and children with disabilities* (p. 19). Helsinki: Ministry of Foreign Affairs of Finland.

Gallagher, K., & Coleman, A. (2009). Visual impairment. In S. Fisher (Ed.), *Teaching exceptional children* (pp. 361–395). Boston, MA: Houghton Mifflin Harcourt Publishing Company.

Gillon, G. T., & Young, A. A. (2002). The phonological awareness skills of children who are blind. *Journal of Visual Impairment & Blindness, 96*(1), 38–49.

Hodkinson, A. (2010). Inclusive and special education in the English educational system: Historical perspectives, recent developments and future challenges. *British Journal of Special Education, 37*(2), 61–67.

International Disability Rights Monitor. (2004). *Regional report for the Americas 2004*. Washington, DC: Center for International Rehabilitation (CIR).

Jenkinson, J. C. (1997). *Mainstream or special: Educating students with disabilities*. London: Routledge Falmer.

Johnsen, B. H. (2001). Curricula for the plurality of individual learning needs: Some thoughts concerning practical innovation towards an inclusive class and school. In B. H. Johnsen & M. D. Skjørten (Eds.), *Education—Special needs education: An Introduction* (pp. 255–303). Oslo: Unipub.

Kamenopoulou, L. (2012). A study on the inclusion of deafblind young people in mainstream schools: Key findings and implications for research and practice. *British Journal of Special Education, 39*(3), 137–145.

Kugelmass, J. W. (2004). *The inclusive school: Sustaining equity and standards*. New York: Teachers College Press.

Kvale, S. (1996). *Interviews: An introduction to Qualitative research interviewing*. Thousand Oaks: Sage.

Miles, S. (2003). *Learning from differences: Understanding community initiatives to improve access to education*. Online, Retrieved May 15, 2017, from www. eenet.org.uk/resources/docs/learning_from diff_yes.pdf

Mitchell, D. (2008). *What really works in special and inclusive education: Using evidence based teaching strategies*. London: Routledge.

Owen, E. O. (2003). *Towards complete compliance with the convention on the rights of the child; An analysis of the laws of Belize*. Belize City: Fer De Lance Productions For United Nation's Children's Fund.

Peters, S. (2003). *Inclusive education: Education for all: Strategy for all children*. New York: Garland.

Rix, J., & Simmons, K. (2005). Introduction: A world of change. In J. Rix, K. Simmons, M. Mind, & K. Sheehy (Eds.), *Policy and power in inclusive education: Values into practice* (pp. 1–10). London: Routledge Falmer.

Sacks, S. Z., & Silberman, R. K. (1998). *Educating students who have visual impairments with other disabilities*. Baltimore: Paul H. Brookes Publishing Co., Inc.

Salisbury, R. (2008). *Teaching pupils with visual impairment: A guide to making the school curriculum accessible.* London: Routledge.

Simon, C., Echeita, G., Sandoval, M., & Lopez, M. (2010). The inclusive educational process of students with visual impairments in Spain: An analysis from the perspective of organization. *Journal of Visual Impairment & Blindness, 104*(9), 565–570.

Smidt, S. (2009). *Introducing Vygotsky: A guide for practitioners and students in early years education.* London: Routledge.

UNESCO. (1994). *The Salamanca statement and framework for action on special needs education.* Paris, France. Retrieved from http://www.unesco.org/education/pdf/SALAMA_E.PDF

UNESCO. (2000). *The Dakar framework for action. Education for all: Meeting our collective commitments.* Dakar, Senegal. Retrieved form http://unesdoc.unesco.org/images/0012/001211/121147e.pdf

UNESCO. (2007). *Caribbean symposium on 'Inclusive Education': Belize report on inclusive education.* Kingston, Jamaica. Retrieved from http://www.ibe.unesco.org/fileadmin/user_upload/Inclusive_Education/Reports/kingston_07/belize_inclusion_07.pdf

UNICEF. (2012). *The situation analysis of children with disabilities.* Belize, Central America: Fer De Lance Productions for United Nations Children's Fund.

Wade, S. E. (2000). *Inclusive education: A casebook and readings for prospective and practicing teachers.* New Jersey: Lawrence Erlbaum.

Webster, A., & Roe, J. (1998). *Children with visual impairment: Social interaction, language and learning.* London: Routledge.

Yin, R. K. (2003). *Case study research: Design and methods.* London: SAGE Publications.

Young, R. (2012). *Situation of children who are visually impaired and blind in Belize.* Belize City: Fer De Lance Productions For United Nation's Children's Fund.

Inclusion and Disability in the Global South: Lessons Learned and Ways Forward

Leda Kamenopoulou

Abstract Chapter 6 is the conclusion and the author provides a critical discussion of key themes and lessons learned from previous chapters in relation to *Inclusion* and *Disability* in Malaysia, Bhutan, Philippines and Belize. Based on the distinction between themes that can be described as generic and thus applicable to many contexts, and those that can only be understood if specific contexts are explored in greater detail, the author proposes a holistic framework for conceptualising *inclusive education* within contexts of the global South and calls for the need to adopt research approaches that are qualitative and flexible, but systematic and reflective. The chapter closes with some specific recommendations for researchers that will also be useful to policy makers and practitioners in the field of inclusive education.

Keywords Inclusive education/inclusion • Global South • Holistic framework • Qualitative research • Sustainable development

L. Kamenopoulou (✉)
University of Roehampton, London, UK

© The Author(s) 2018
L. Kamenopoulou (ed.), *Inclusive Education and Disability in the Global South*, https://doi.org/10.1007/978-3-319-72829-2_6

6.1   Overview of Final Chapter

In this final chapter I provide a critical discussion of key themes in relation to inclusion and disability that emerged from all chapters, and I outline important lessons that can be learned from the research on four global South countries that was presented in this book. To begin with, it is hard not to notice that some of the key themes emerging from the chapters can be described as *generic*, meaning that they *are* or *can be* applicable to many contexts, whereas others can only be seen as extremely *context-specific*, meaning that they are only pertinent to particular contexts and their characteristics. On the basis of this observation, I argue that it is possible to propose a way of conceptualising *inclusion* in global South contexts that is holistic, and helps researchers, policy makers and practitioners organise and understand the various concepts and debates related to inclusion in education in these contexts. This conceptual framework is based on the simple but fundamental distinction between inclusive concepts, issues, etc. that are generic, and those that can only be known or understood if some specific contexts are explored in greater detail. In closing, I outline some recommendations for researchers in the field of inclusion and disability in the global South that will also be useful to practitioners and policy makers.

6.2   Context Specific Themes and the Value of Qualitative Research

In line with the aims of this book, its chapters brought to light some rare knowledge gathered following research on inclusion and disability within four global South contexts on which very little is known. The studies presented highlighted some key issues, challenges and opportunities for inclusion and disability that are particular to Malaysia, Bhutan, Philippines and Belize.

For example, an understanding of disability that is influenced by religious and philosophical beliefs about karma in Bhutan was an important finding that emerged from the research presented in Chap. 3; and it illustrates how the meaning of inclusive education and disability can be extremely context specific. By referring to the Convention on the Rights of Persons with Disabilities (CRPD) and the Western models of conceptualising disability when exploring how Bhutanese people understood *inclusion* and *disability*, Dukpa & Kamenopoulou demonstrated that the particular cultural characteristics of the Bhutanese context, namely, the mutual influences between modern educational discourses and traditional Buddhist principles, shape and create a quite unique understanding of these concepts that can be very different from current global North definitions. In his ethnographic study on disability in Bhutanese society, Schuelka (2012) explains that a range of factors have influenced the recent big changes in Bhutan's education system, including major UN-led human rights initiatives signed by the government of Bhutan, educational policies imported from India, and input from international organisations like UNICEF who currently work in collaboration with the Ministry of Education to help modernise the education system and to establish approaches based on human rights discourses. At the same time, 'medical experts' from abroad introduce a medical discourse when advising local professionals in Bhutan (Schuelka, 2015). All these external influences continue to coexist with Buddhist views about disability as someone's fate, which can be argued to place the blame on the disabled person, but still have the power to influence the way disability is understood and conceptualised in modern Bhutan. However, it must be emphasised that values such as the principle of GNH reflect inclusive values, and in this sense, inclusive education is not something imposed to Bhutan from outside but part and parcel of its aspirations for an inclusive society (Dorji & Schuelka, 2016; Kamenopoulou & Dukpa, 2017). Given the above it might be necessary to question for example the usefulness of global North-bred 'experts' on inclusion, who 'scurry the world for meetings, research and consultancy' (Grech, 2015: p. 13), when inclusion and disability are fluid concepts that can be understood at the local level in many different ways, can take different meanings depending on the particular context, and can be shaped by the complex interactions between factors like education background, social class, economic status, religious and cultural beliefs. Instead, Chap. 3 calls for more research and a better understanding of the conceptualisation of inclusion and disability within local contexts that still remain largely unexplored.

Religion or belonging to a religious group emerged as an important factor mediating one's experiences of disability and inclusion or exclusion from the research on the interplay of deafness and ethnicity in the process of identity development presented in Chap. 2. Pregel & Kamenopoulou highlighted the uniqueness of the Malaysian society in terms of its plurality of ethnicities, religions and languages. Interestingly, this research found that the identities of the four Malaysian deaf people who took part in the interviews were more clearly shaped by their disability status and as a result, any experiences of exclusion or discrimination were primarily associated to the deafness aspect of their identity. However, it also emerged very strongly that other factors such as religion could play a protective role against social isolation and this was the case for those Malay deaf people who were Christian and tended to receive more support for accessing religious activities and events compared to those participants who were Muslim. This highlights again how one's experiences of inclusion or exclusion can be extremely context specific and dependent upon arrangements and norms existing within a particular society.

Similarly, context-specific factors also emerged from the research presented in Chap. 4, were Villamero & Kamenopoulou highlighted the barriers posed to teachers in terms of implementing inclusive approaches to the assessment of children with disabilities. In the context of the Philippines, extreme poverty and social inequality can hamper teachers' efforts to be more inclusive in their teaching and can take the form of large class sizes and lack of resources. However, the three teachers who took part in the research showed a clear commitment to inclusion and reported using innovative approaches in order to meet the assessment needs of all learners in their classrooms. This highlights the role of positive teacher attitudes and creative initiatives in the implementation of inclusion that can be the basis for a 'success story' of inclusive education, as was the case here: despite really challenging circumstances, teachers in our research were creative and for example used peer support when scaffolding tasks as an alternative to adult-led support due to the large class sizes; and they described how they continuously made adaptations to any existing resources because of the lack of necessary or more high tech materials.

Similarly, in Chap. 5, Azueta & Kamenopoulou explored Belize teachers' views about including children with Visual Impairment (VI) in their classrooms and stressed the lack of resources that are specifically designed for these children's learning, like Braille, as well as the lack of on-going teacher support offered in this context by professionals, who are more skilled in methods used to communicate with and to teach children with VI. With the only teacher trainer available in the country based in Belize City, the authors pointed out how teachers in rural areas of Belize lack real opportunities to gain knowledge, training, and skills necessary for including pupils with VI in mainstream classrooms.

All the above are examples of issues that are context-specific, and provide a strong argument for the need to conduct research that is able to capture the subtle characteristics of a particular context and to gather the narratives of those living within this context, in order to give them a voice and shed light to their unique realities and perspectives. Barton (1997) argues for the need to listen to the context, in which inclusive education is expected to take place, and stresses the importance of allowing voices from that context to be heard. Booth (1999) stresses the value of comparative and qualitative research in terms of providing *'instructive lessons from all practice'* (p. 165), especially in the case of voices that are too rarely heard. Qualitative research like the studies presented in this book can capture these subtleties, but this type of research remains scarce and as a result many contexts remain unexplored and in reality, silenced. Grech (2015) puts it eloquently:

> It is no secret that qualitative research humanising, prioritising, listening to and articulating the voices of disabled people in extreme poverty –research unafraid of the 'uncontrollableness' of data/life—remains perilously scarce. (p. 15)

He moreover writes about lack of qualitative research collecting narratives from rural areas and indigenous populations, whose particular needs and characteristics slip through the net of *'aggregated data in a complex terrain of intersectionalities'* (p. 15). The need to allow silenced voices and contexts to be heard was the main rationale behind including in this book research that explored disability and inclusion in contexts of the global South through a qualitative lens and focused on under-researched issues and perspectives. Moreover, all studies presented in this book were conducted *'in a systematic and self-critical manner'* (Farrell & Aiscow, 2002: p. 9) and were based on solid methodological and ethical frameworks. From the more unstructured approach of the research conducted in Malaysia that was participatory and ethnographic in nature, to the more structured and interview based research conducted in Belize, Bhutan and the Philippines, all studies presented in this book were conducted in a systematic, transparent and self-critical manner. It is important to stress that the way in which a research is conducted is of crucial importance, and Grech finds little value in the scarce qualitative research on disability and the global South that exists today:

> For many theorists, the global South remains an object of fleeting curiosity and 'occasional study' [...] From this position, all the world is made to look the same, simplified, reduced and homogenised. (2013: p. 90)

[T]here is also too little reflection on methods, approaches and positionalty. This includes increasingly field-distant and isolated 'professionals' sending unknowing research assistants unfamiliar with the community [...] with a piece of paper drafted miles away. (2015: p. 15)

It needs to be emphasised that the researchers who carried out the studies presented in this book all left the comfort of their offices and experienced the research settings in real life, thus generating much needed knowledge and gathering some thus far silenced voices. In relation to *researcher positionality* more specifically, it is interesting to note that the first authors of Chaps. 3, 4 and 5 were also insiders in relation to their topic, in the sense that they were professionals, who prior to conducting research, had spent all their lives in these contexts and had experienced first hand some of the issues they were researching whilst being part of the education system over many years. The first author of Chap. 2, on the other hand was clearly an outsider in the local deaf community, where he conducted his ethnographic research. In all four studies researcher *reflexivity* and *positionality* played a central role throughout. For example, the first author of Chap. 3 reflected and acted on the possible bias i.e. the possibility that the three teachers from Negros Oriental in the Philippines who took part in the study may have had the tendency to please him with their responses during the interviews and to respond in ways that they thought he expected them to respond or he would have liked them to respond. It goes without saying that a self-reflective approach like this one has many advantages both ethically and methodologically.

In contrast, the first author of Chap. 2, who is originally from Italy, was faced with subtle dilemmas owing to his identity as a white, male, middle class, European researcher, who was so visibly an outsider in the eyes of his local research participants. Being aware of his position and role when conducting outsider research, upon arrival in Penang, he took classes in the Malaysian Sign Language. Learning the local sign language proved to be a powerful research strategy, because it helped him interact with potential participants, but also to gain their acceptance as an outsider. Furthermore, it helped him identify participants and gatekeepers by coming into contact with Deaf organisations, interpreters, teachers, and Deaf advocates. In a nutshell, being acutely aware of his own identity and differences, he spent a lot of time mixing within the local community, visiting local schools and familiarising himself with the research context.

Future researchers can learn valuable lessons from this sensitive and reflective approach to conducting outsider research, especially in light of arguments against the colonisation of disability studies by the West or 'academic neo-imperialism' (for an excellent discussion of this phenomenon, see Grech, 2015).

To sum up, with its focus on under-researched contexts and under-represented voices, this book makes a valuable addition to the current knowledge base on inclusion and disability in countries of the global South as viewed from the perspective of those who live in these contexts. Perhaps more importantly, it reinforces the argument for the need to adopt research designs that are flexible and qualitative in nature, but also systematic, transparent and self-reflective. For only this type of research is able to capture subtle contextual differences and characteristics, and to give priority to the voices of the locals over the researcher's a priori assumptions.

6.3   GENERIC THEMES

At the same time as identifying context-specific issues, readers who are familiar with the broader field of inclusive education and disability were surely able to identify some central themes that are repeatedly found in the relevant literature and that emerged from more than one of the studies presented this book. For example, the lack of teacher training for inclusive education was a finding that was common from the studies in Bhutan and Belize. As I have written before (see Kamenopoulou, Buli-Holmberg, & Siska, 2015), the education of teachers for inclusive education remains a huge question mark at universal level and as a result, teacher preparation for inclusive education has recently been gaining a lot of interest internationally. Erten and Savage (2012) argue that there is a dearth of study programmes providing teachers with knowledge on inclusive education and moreover stress that this is a global issue. The gaps in teacher preparation for inclusive education have also been reported as an issue facing global North contexts, such as England (Frood, 2011). These gaps are problematic, because there is a considerable body of research literature suggesting that preparing teachers for inclusive education supports its successful implementation in practice (see for example Boyle, Topping, & Jindal-Snape, 2013; Cameron & Jotveit, 2014; Cologon, 2012; Holmberg & Tangen, 2001). Hence the development of inclusive teachers is an essential ingredient of the successful implementation of inclusive education and it is an issue that needs to be prioritised at the global level.

Another generic theme that emerged was the stark contradiction between policy and practice or *rhetoric* and *reality*. It was shown that in more than one of the contexts researched, like Philippines and Bhutan, there are policy initiatives and programmes in place that set the framework for inclusive education, but in reality the contexts are inadequately prepared or unable to implement inclusive education in practice. This is another recurring theme occupying a central place in the literature about inclusive education policy globally (see Carnovali, 2017; Watkins & Meijer, 2016) so much so that Schuelka (2012) argues that persistently pointing out the gaps between policy and practice *'is no longer helpful research'* (p. 152). Hansen (2012) goes even further to suggest that accepting the gaps between the vision of inclusion and its achievement in practice can be: *'a pragmatic solution to the relationship between a conceptual understanding of inclusion as a limitless principle and an a priori assumption that inclusion in practice always has its limits'* (p. 92).

Even if it is useful to accept the limits that inclusive education may have in practice, it is noteworthy that the research presented in this book confirmed the existence or consideration of well-designed policy blueprints, but inadequate practices or simply put, it confirmed the distance between *rhetoric* and *reality*. In this case it can be argued that more research is needed on why specific global North-led initiatives such as for example the Convention on the Rights of Persons with Disabilities (CRPD) or the Sustainable Development Goals (SDG), in practice still face great challenges in some contexts, and especially those of the global South. Perhaps therefore the most important lesson learned from all chapters is that researchers and policy makers at national and international level must listen more to the voices and perspectives of the people living in countries of the global South, and especially their experiences and views about inclusion and disability within their very unique contexts. The main argument here is that greater cross-cultural sensitivity and understanding are warranted. Given these points, in the next section I propose a way of conceptualising inclusive education that can lead to more meaningful and helpful research approaches, and more realistic and grounded inclusive policies and practices especially in global South contexts.

6.4   Towards a Holistic Way for Conceptualising Inclusive Education

Based on the simple observation that some findings emerging from the research presented in this book were only applicable to specific contexts, whereas others seemed to apply more generally to more than one contexts, it is possible to see an emerging pattern, which could be thought of as a way of conceptualising inclusive education or inclusion in education. I argue that this simple theoretical framework is a useful tool that allows us to organise the numerous concepts and issues relating to inclusive education within the global South (and beyond) and helps logically structure the various confusing debates pertaining to it. I present a summary of what the proposed framework looks like in Table 6.1.

In a nutshell, on the one hand there are generic concepts and issues that I have called *Universals*. These generic concepts and issues would seem to apply to all or most contexts. Inclusive values based on human rights such as the right of all children to education or the right of disabled people to equal opportunities would fall under this category. Similarly, issues like the big gaps in the preparation of teachers for inclusive education can also be described as a more or less universal problem facing countries in the realisation of inclusive education at the moment. On the other hand, *Singulars* are concepts and issues that seem to only apply to specific contexts and depend on particular contextual characteristics. Concepts, values and cultural beliefs that are specific to a given context, such as the understanding of disability from a karmic model seen in Bhutan or the lack of resources

Table 6.1 'Holistic framework' for conceptualising inclusive education in the global South

UNIVERSALS	Concepts	Inclusive principles based on human rights	Right to education Right to equal opportunities
	Issues	Gaps in the development of inclusive education and barriers to its implementation	Unpreparedness of teachers Gaps between policy and practice
SINGULARS	Concepts	Own principles and values, cultural beliefs	Own understanding of disability, inclusion, rights, equality
	Issues	Context specific gaps and barriers	Poverty, social inequality, corruption

in some of the poorest contexts like Belize and Philippines, would belong to this category. Similarly, other issues that are be associated with specific contextual characteristics of countries of the global South such as extreme poverty or social and economic inequality can be seen as purely context specific.

The above 'holistic' framework can be a useful tool for conceptualising, understanding and researching concepts and issues in relation to inclusive education, especially within contexts of the global South that have very particular characteristics. Using this framework, *Universals* like all children's right to education cannot be overlooked and must be monitored and safeguarded in all contexts, despite their differences. At the same time, because the very notion of 'right' for example can acquire different meanings depending on the cultural context (Miles, 2000), it is necessary and helpful to explore in depth and gain a greater understanding of specific local realities. Grech (2011) reminds us that *'first of all any discussion about rights must emphasise that these are a Western invention'* (p. 91) and that *'in the overriding presence of poverty and deprivation, rights more often than not run the risk of being utopian, and inattention to local contexts, political economies, histories and cultures may make them contextually insignificant'* (p. 92). Moreover, human rights are safeguarded through UN's work, but in reality this work includes *'unstable coalitions of governments, bureaucracies and NGOs'* (Connell, 2011: p. 1378). In global South countries, Connell explains, NGOs often end up being the sole advocates of rights agendas, but unfortunately they too *'are constrained by the neoliberal environment from which they are funded, and are influenced by the professional cultures of the global North'* (p. 1378). Therefore getting a parallel insight into the *Singulars* allows silenced voices to be heard and encourages greater sensitivity towards and understanding of local contexts and perspectives. Thus using this framework, researchers, policy makers and practitioners can remain alert to some of the very particular characteristics of countries of the global South that shape the course of inclusive education in these contexts, such as for example the huge social inequalities or the continued marginalisation and invisibility of disabled people within these contexts.

6.5   WAYS FORWARD: RECOMMENDATIONS FOR RESEARCH

Based on my discussion of all chapters and the holistic framework for conceptualising inclusive education in contexts of the global South that I outlined in the previous section, as a way forward I suggest that inclusive education research should focus on the following key priorities:

1. Gathering data that will help confirm and further explore the *Universals* or generic themes of inclusion in global South (and North) contexts. For example, researchers should focus on exploring the specific gaps between policy and practice in different countries or on identifying the exact areas for further development in the organisation of provision for teacher training on inclusive education. Moreover, as mentioned earlier, in some contexts there are still big gaps in the information available regarding inclusive education and disability, more specifically. Miles and Singal (2010) stress that some of the poorest and most marginalised children have been overlooked and as a result there is a striking lack of data on the education of those groups, especially in regions like South America. Hence more research is needed in relation to universal issues that relate to inclusive education, such as for example if and how the right of all children to free primary education is safeguarded everywhere, and especially within under-researched contexts. Data gathered on these universal issues could then become a list of international key priorities for policy and practice.

2. Gathering data that provides rich insights into the *Singulars*. Grech (2015) talks about the lack of empirical research on countries of the global South and emhpasises the '*virtual absence of regional and country specific research*'(p. 14) on South America and the Caribbean. Obtaining a more accurate perspective of these underexplored contexts can be achieved by capturing the unique experiences of local people, e.g. teachers, parents, children and young people, policy makers and teacher trainers, collected through qualitative and context sensitive research, conducted in a systematic and self-critical manner. For example, certain context specific factors like poverty, lack of resources or negative societal attitudes that may contribute to the greater marginalisation of people with disabilities in countries of the global South, as well as the complex intersections between these factors need to be explored in more depth. Data gathered on context specific issues could then become a list of national or regional key priorities in relation to the policy and practice of inclusive education, priorities that have been set using an actual 'bottom up' approach.

3. Creating opportunities for local research to flourish. One of the aims of this book was to contribute to the decentralisation of global North-generated theories and knowledge and in this way to assist in

the decolonisation of studies on the global South. By presenting a collection of research on inclusive education and disability conducted in countries of the global South, on which very little is known, this book gave a voice to education professionals from different backgrounds, who took a leading role in undertaking the research as part of their post-graduate studies, and allowed them to share their knowledge of the possibilities and challenges for inclusive education and disability in their specific contexts. All these researchers conducted culturally sensitive and reflective research, and the result was far more valuable that the simple reproduction of global North ideas *'that leave the knowledge system unchallenged and unchanged'* (Grech, 2015: p. 17). Ultimately, what this book has shown is that it is important to find ways of encouraging local researchers to conduct more studies within their under-explored contexts. These can take the form of more funding and programmes for local teachers or other education professionals, who wish to undertake further studies and research on inclusive education; funding for research projects that specifically focus on disability and inclusion within neglected contexts of the global South; and partnerships between local Universities and schools. Such initiatives would empower the people of the global South and would allow them to have their own voices heard in relation to what needs to be done for the development of inclusive education in their contexts to be *successful* and *sustainable*.

REFERENCES

Barton, L. (1997). Inclusive education: Romantic, subversive or realistic? *International Journal of Inclusive Education, 1*(3), 231–242.

Booth, T. (1999). Viewing inclusion from a distance: Gaining perspective from comparative study. *Support for Learning, 14*(4), 164–168.

Boyle, C., Topping, C., & Jindal-Snape, D. (2013). Teachers' attitudes towards inclusion in high schools. *Teachers and Teaching: Theory and Practice, 19*(5), 527–542.

Cameron, D. L., & Jortveit, M. (2014). Do different routes to becoming a special educator produce different understandings of the profession and its core concepts? *European Journal of Special Needs Education, 29*(4), 559–570.

Carnovali, S. (2017). The right to inclusive education of persons with disabilities in Italy. Reflections and perspectives. *Athens Journal of Education (special issue on 'Inclusive Education'), 4*(4), 315–326.

Cologon, K. (2012). Confidence in their own ability: Postgraduate early child-hood students examining their attitudes towards inclusive education. *International Journal of Inclusive Education, 16*(11), 1155–1173.

Connell, R. (2011). Southern bodies and disability: Re-thinking concepts. *Third World Quarterly, 32*(8), 1369–1381.

Dorji, R., & Schuelka, M. J. (2016). Children with disabilities in Bhutan: Transitioning from special educational needs to inclusive education. In M. J. Schuelka & T. W. Maxwell (Eds.), *Education in Bhutan: Culture, schooling and gross national happiness* (pp. 181–198). Singapore: Springer Science.

Erten, O., & Savage, R. S. (2012). Moving forward in inclusive education research. *International Journal of Inclusive Education, 162*, 221–233.

Farrell, P., & Ainscow, M. (2002). Making special education inclusive: Mapping the issues. In P. Farrell & M. Ainscow (Eds.), *Making special education inclusive* (pp. 1–12). London: David Fulton.

Frood, K. (2011). The green paper—A view from mainstream. *Journal of Research in Special Educational Needs, 12*(2), 115–117.

Grech, S. (2011). Recolonising debates or perpetuated coloniality? Decentring the spaces of disability, development and community in the global South. *International Journal of Inclusive Education, 15*(1), 87–100.

Grech, S. (2013). Disability, childhood and poverty: Critical perspectives on Guatemala. In T. Curran & K. Runswick-Cole (Eds.), *Disabled children's childhood studies: Critical approaches in a global context* (pp. 89–104). Basingstoke: Palgrave Macmillan.

Grech, S. (2015). *Disability and poverty in the global South: Renegotiating development in Guatemala*. London: Palgrave Macmillan.

Hansen, J. H. (2012). Limits to inclusion. *International Journal of Inclusive Education, 16*(1), 89–98.

Holmberg, J. B., & Tangen, R. (Eds.). (2001). Noen komplikasjoner for framtidig kompetanseutvikling [The need for expertice development in schools] In *Kompetanseutvikling og fleksibel læring. Erfaringer og behov for spesialpedagogisk utdanning i videregående skole* [*Competence building and flexible learning. The need for special education expertise in high school*] (pp. 180–189). Blindern: Institutt for spesialpedagogikk.

Kamenopoulou, L., Buli-Holmberg, J., & Siska, J. (2015). An exploration of student teachers' perspectives at the start of a post-graduate study programme on inclusion and special needs education. *International Journal of Inclusive Education, 20*(7), 743–755.

Kamenopoulou, L., & Dukpa, D. (2017). Karma and human rights: Bhutanese teachers' perspectives on inclusion and disability. *International Journal of Inclusive Education*. https://doi.org/10.1080/13603116.2017.1365274

Miles, M. (2000). Disability on a different model: Glimpses of an Asian heritage. *Disability & Society, 15*(4), 603–618.

Miles, S., & Singal, N. (2010). Education for all and inclusive education debate: Conflict, contradiction, or opportunity? *International Journal of Inclusive Education, 14*(1), 14–15.

Schuelka, M. J. (2012). Inclusive education in Bhutan: A small state with alternative priorities. *Current Issues in Comparative Education, 15*(1), 145–156.

Schuelka, M. J. (2015). The evolving construction and conceptualisation of 'disability' in Bhutan. *Disability & Society, 30*(6), 820–833.

Watkins, A., & Meijer, C. J. W. (Vol., Eds.). (2016). Implementing inclusive education: Issues in bridging the policy-practice gap. In C. Forlin (Series Ed.), *International perspectives on inclusive education* (Vol. 8). Emerald Publishing Limited.

INDEX

© The Author(s) 2018   143
L. Kamenopoulou (ed.), *Inclusive Education and Disability in the*
Global South, https://doi.org/10.1007/978-3-319-72829-2

W
Wangchuk, Jigma Singye (Druk
Gyalpo), 57
Western
countries, 27
deaf communities, 27
education, 63
ideas, 10
literature, 63

theories, 7
Wheelchairs, 58
Work environments, 41
World Health Organisation (WHO), 3

Z
Zone of Proximal Development
(ZPD), 98

CPSIA information can be obtained
at www.ICGtesting.com
Printed in the USA
LVOW13*1922270318
571334LV00013B/297/P